Computer Repair with Diagnostic Flowcharts

Third Edition

Troubleshooting PC Hardware Problems from Boot

Failure to Poor Performance

Morris Rosenthal

Please Read

The author has done his best to provide accurate and up-to-date information in this book, but he cannot guarantee that the information is correct or will fit your particular situation. The book is sold with the understanding that the publisher and the author are not engaged in rendering professional or engineering services. If expert assistance is required, the services of a competent professional should be sought.

Flowcharts produced with Microsoft Visio Standard

Published by Foner Books

www.fonerbooks.com

ISBN 0-9723801-8-3

Table of Contents

A special thanks to Tracie Shea for three editions worth of struggling with my prose and typos.

Also by the author:

The Laptop Repair Workbook

Start Your Own Computer Business

For additional troubleshooting material see:

www.fonerbooks.com

and

www.ifitjams.com

Instructions

This book was not designed to be read from cover to cover. At the core of the book are seventeen diagnostic flowcharts, and the sole purpose of the text is to expand upon them. The flowcharts themselves are necessarily written in short-hand form, to fit a meaningful number of decision points on a page. A linear text is simply not possible due to the decision tree structure of the flowcharts. The diamond shape for each decision point in the flowchart is repeated in the outer margin of the pages following the flowchart. This marks the section of text that explains the action in more detail. Do not read beyond the designated section without returning to the flowchart to determine the next step.

The ovals in the flowcharts contain instructions or suggestions. If a suggestion like "reseat the cable" doesn't work, the best course may be to return to the previous decision point and continue with the diagnostic down the other branch. These charts are designed to push parts swapping to the end of the diagnostic procedures wherever possible, so readers without a stock of spare parts will have the best chance to repair the problem without spending money. You should always label any parts you remove from a machine as "suspicious," and if it becomes apparent that they are truly faulty, dispose of them.

The "home plate" symbol is used in flowcharts to transfer control to an off-chart point. Some of the flowcharts in this book have multiple decision paths that will send you to a different flowchart for a different hardware sub-system. As with the suggestion oval, if you've already been there, you can retreat to the last decision point and determine if following the other branch makes sense.

Diagnosis is an art. There's no point in having the world's leading brain surgeon poking around in your skull if the problem is with your liver. This is exactly analogous to what happens when techs or hobbyists troubleshoot PCs without following some intelligent diagnostic procedure. The most experienced techs are sometimes some of the worst diagnosticians, because they're overconfident in their troubleshooting abilities. If you work on a given brand of PCs for a few years and you find that 90% of the problems encountered are due to a bad power supply, you start attributing all PC problems to power supplies. If you'd been working in a different shop on a different brand, you may have concluded that 90% of all computer problems were due to bad RAM, etc. You should always approach each new problem with an open mind and look at the most basic possibilities before jumping to conclusions.

This book focuses on ATX PCs with a modern plug-n-play motherboard and BIOS. These PCs first appeared in the mid-90's and still account for all of the standard PCs sold today. ATX computers are turned off and on by a switch on the front panel of the PC which tells the motherboard to instruct the power supply to come full on. An ATX power supply is always supplying a trickle of current to the motherboard as long as it's plugged in and the override switch on the back of the supply isn't turned off. To avoid the risk of damaging components when working in the PC, unplug the power supply before making any changes inside the case.

Since unplugging the PC removes the ground, this increases the risk of damaging components with a static electric discharge. In over 25 years of working on PCs I've only zapped one component that I know of, a SCSI hard drive, and that was in a high static environment. Don't work in a dry area with a rug or rub Styrofoam all over your body before picking up a part. Don't work in an area where you frequently experience static electric shocks. It's good to form the habit of touching some exposed piece of metal, even if it's not grounded itself, before picking up static sensitive devices. If you don't have much experience working around computer parts and the static threat worries you, buy a static bracelet and tether at the local electronics store for a few dollars.

You need to have a basic knowledge of the terminology of computers and the physical appearance of PC components to benefit from these flowcharts. This book is not for beginners, but we have added links to illustrated procedures on the publisher's website, fonerbooks.com. Many of the procedures described in this book require a basic knowledge of working with electronics. Procedures describing live power and bench testing may result in harm to the computer hardware, the tester (you), and the environment (your house).

The vast majority of ATX PCs run some version of Microsoft Windows. Therefore, when it's necessary to refer to the operating system, the references are usually to Device Manager, the standard Windows hardware manager through Windows 8 and likely beyond.

For non-gamers, hardware obsolescence is primarily driven by operating systems software, not by performance or applications. As Microsoft abandons support for Windows XP, tens of millions of computer users running older PCs with Windows XP will decide that the security risk of running XP on the Internet is too great. Without frequent patches from Microsoft to correct known vulnerabilities, many people will stop using these otherwise perfectly serviceable PCs if they can't be easily upgraded to Windows 7 or 8.

In revising this book for the third edition, we kept support for obsolete hardware to the extent that space allows. In some instances, the newer PCs are much simpler from a hardware perspective than the older PCs, so there was no need to drop troubleshooting steps to make room for newer, more common hardware issues. However, if you have a ten year old PC you are trying to troubleshoot and you don't want to read about SATA drives and quad-core processors, you can always pick up a cheap first edition of this book through a second-hand bookstore.

In some cases, we use the traditional terminology to describe current hardware that has evolved beyond the term. A good example is "CMOS Setup," the expression most technicians use to refer to nonvolatile settings stored for the BIOS to control basic motherboard operations. Newer motherboards don't actually use battery backed CMOS memory to store these settings, but the terminology survives. And we use commonly interchanged terminology, like PCI Express vs. PCIe, in both forms, since people use the former when talking and the latter when texting.

Power Supply (PSU) Failure

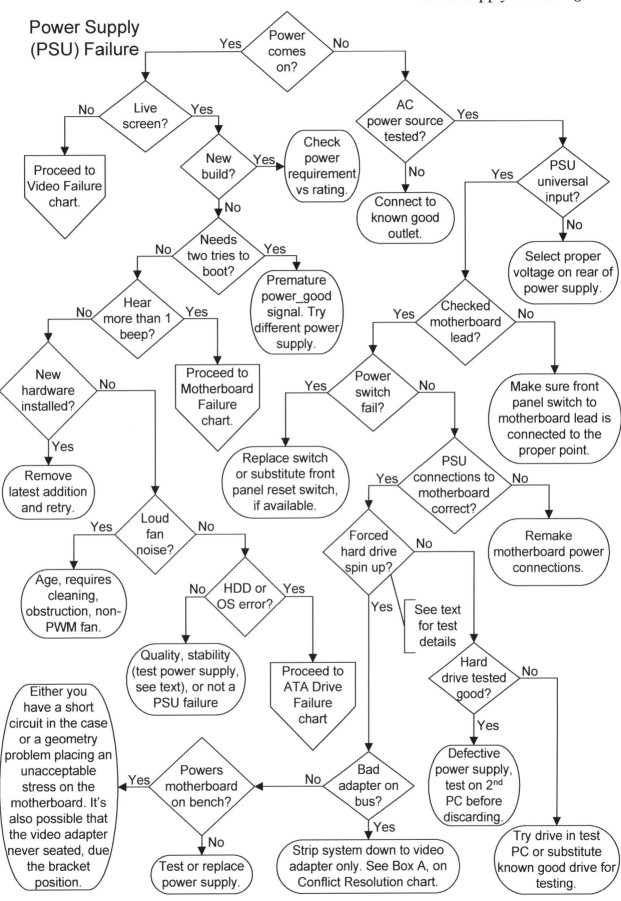

Power comes on?

Yes → **Live screen?**
- No → Proceed to Video Failure chart.
- Yes → **New build?**
  - Yes → Check power requirement vs rating.
  - No → **Needs two tries to boot?**
    - Yes → Premature power_good signal. Try different power supply.
    - No → **Hear more than 1 beep?**
      - Yes → Proceed to Motherboard Failure chart.
      - No → **New hardware installed?**
        - Yes → Remove latest addition and retry.
        - No → **Loud fan noise?**
          - Yes → Age, requires cleaning, obstruction, non-PWM fan.
          - No → **HDD or OS error?**
            - No → Quality, stability (test power supply, see text), or not a PSU failure
            - Yes → Proceed to ATA Drive Failure chart

No → **AC power source tested?**
- No → Connect to known good outlet.
- Yes → **PSU universal input?**
  - No → Select proper voltage on rear of power supply.
  - Yes → **Checked motherboard lead?**
    - Yes → **Power switch fail?**
      - Yes → Replace switch or substitute front panel reset switch, if available.
      - No → **PSU connections to motherboard correct?**
        - Yes → **Forced hard drive spin up?**
          - Yes → Bad adapter on bus?
          - No → See text for test details → **Hard drive tested good?**
            - Yes → Defective power supply, test on 2nd PC before discarding.
            - No → Try drive in test PC or substitute known good drive for testing.
        - No → Remake motherboard power connections.
    - No → Make sure front panel switch to motherboard lead is connected to the proper point.

Bad adapter on bus?
- No → **Powers motherboard on bench?**
  - Yes → Either you have a short circuit in the case or a geometry problem placing an unacceptable stress on the motherboard. It's also possible that the video adapter never seated, due the bracket position.
  - No → Test or replace power supply.
- Yes → Strip system down to video adapter only. See Box A, on Conflict Resolution chart.

Power Supply Failure

The first step in the troubleshooting process is simply determining if the power supply is coming on. You can usually hear the mechanical components in PCs that make rotational noise when they are powered up. Noise makers include the hard drive, as its electric motor spins up the platters, and plenty of fan noise is normal for PCs without PWM (Pulse Width Modulation) fans. Your PC should also give a single beep if it passes its internal start-up diagnostic, and there are always status LED's to tell you the system is on, though some home PC builders don't bother connecting them. If your hearing isn't good, you can check to see if the power supply fan is creating a breeze. Monitors are powered independently, so unless you're looking at a notebook PC, a live screen doesn't indicate a working power supply.

If power isn't coming on, take the time to double check that the cord is plugged into a live socket and firmly seated in the back of the power supply. You don't need a DVM (Digital Volt Meter) to check your power outlet. Unplug the power supply cord from the outlet and plug a working lamp into the very same socket to test it. Don't assume that all the sockets in a power strip are working just because the power strip status light is lit. I'm always coming across power strips with one or more bad outlets. The power supply cord is basically bullet-proof, unless you cut through it with something, but if the PC gets moved or the cord gets kicked, it's easy for that cord to pull out a bit from the socket on the back of the power supply and still look like it's plugged in.

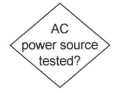

Newer, high quality power supplies are generally termed "universal input" or "full range" and will work on any AC voltage from 90V to 240V at 50 Hz or 60 Hz. While supply voltage shouldn't be an issue with a previously working PC, if you've replaced the power supply or moved the system, it's always a possibility. Older power supplies shipped with a manual switch to select the correct voltage (110V/ 220V). This small red slide switch is located on the back of the power supply, usually between the power cord and the on/off override. You should always unplug the power supply cord before changing the voltage because modern ATX power supplies are always live when plugged in. While it's not recommended that you experiment, if you plug the power supply with the switch on 220V into the socket in a 110V country like the U.S., it may still work when you correct the voltage. But if you power on a supply

set for 110V in a country with a 220V distribution, you'll probably blow the power supply fuse (at the very least), and potentially damage the supply and the connected components.

One obvious reason the PC won't turn on when you press the switch is if the switch lead has separated from the motherboard. This lead is usually labeled PW-ON or PW and it reaches from the front the PC case to a small block of metallic pins for case connections to the motherboard. It's not at all uncommon to encounter this problem if you've done any work inside the case because the leads aren't glued in place and the connectors aren't tight. Even if you've built a number of PCs in your life, it's normal to get this connection wrong when you replace or install a new motherboard due to poor identification of the pins in the connector block. On the bright side, it's a non-polarized switch so you only have to pick the correct two pins, not the orientation. I've come across cases where the printed book that ships with a new motherboard disagrees with the printing on the motherboard itself as to the function of different pin sets in the connector block. I always go with the motherboard labeling in those cases.

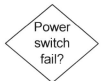

Check that the power switch is really working by using a meter on the continuity setting, or just check for a short when the switch is closed if your meter only measures Ohms. ATX technology PCs don't switch the line voltage, as did the previous generation AT power supplies. The switch is just a binary logic input for the motherboard which is always partially live in an ATX system that's plugged in. The motherboard follows its programming to tell the power supply to come on full or to shut down, depending on the settings. The same switch may be used to wake the PC from stand-by mode. This doesn't apply to obsolete AT PCs, where you'll see the heavy power cord going to a large switch, but those systems are pretty much gone.

When I'm troubleshooting the power switch in an ATX system and I don't have a meter with me, I just short across the two pins for the power switch in the motherboard connector block with a screwdriver to see if the system will start. Since it's a live power test, don't try it if you aren't comfortable working with live equipment and might jerk away in surprise when the power does come on. You could end up stabbing the motherboard or the video adapter with the screwdriver, just from reflexes, and do serious damage. When you encounter a failed switch and don't have a replacement on hand, you may be able to scavenge the hard reset switch present on older cases.

If you believe the motherboard was badly damaged by a power surge or a short, it's possible the switch circuit has failed or that the power supply is immediately shutting off to protect itself from a high current draw. Another live power test for experienced technicians is to bypass the motherboard switching circuit by disconnecting all of the power supply leads to the motherboard and then shorting the green P_On lead to a black ground lead in a standard 20 or 24 pin ATX power supply connector. But switching power supplies require a load to operate so you must keep the hard drive connected.

If you press in the power switch on your system and it doesn't immediately shut off the PC, that's how ATX systems are supposed to work. The power switch is programmable and the action can often be defined in CMOS Setup or Windows. The normal setting for PC power switches makes you hold the switch in for three to five seconds to shut down the system. Pressing the switch for a shorter duration might put the system in sleep mode or wake it up from hibernation, important options for power conservation. If Windows fails to turn off the power when you select "shut down," it's usually due to a corrupted file or bad setting in the operating system. The first thing to try is running "System Restore" to a date prior to when the problem appeared. Windows may also fail to shut down if an external USB device, often a back-up hard drive, has been installed without the proper software drivers or is sharing a USB port. It's easy enough to troubleshoot USB shut down issues by disconnecting those devices one at a time.

Modern motherboards require multiple connections from the power supply, starting with the main 24 pin ATX connector that replaced the older 20 pin connector in most designs. Power hungry CPUs and chipsets have led to a variety of supplemental connectors, including a 4 pin or 8 pin ATX 12V supply on many systems, and multiple 6 pin PCIe connectors for serious graphics cards. With the power supply unplugged, make sure all motherboard connectors are properly seated and latched by removing them and reattaching. I've always found the standard latching system for the main power connector to be counter-intuitive. It works kind of like a see-saw with a pivot, you have to squeeze in at the top to pop it open at the bottom. They usually don't make any noise on releasing, but you should get a satisfying click when you remake the connection.

PSU connections to motherboard correct?

ATX Version 2.2 - 24 wire motherboard connector

Pin 1	Pin 2	Pin 3	Pin 4	Pin 5	Pin 6	Pin 7	Pin 8	Pin 9	Pin 10	Pin 11	Pin 12
3.3 V	3.3V	Gnd	5V	Gnd	5V	Gnd	P _ O K	5VSB	12V	12V	3.3V
Oran	Oran	Blk	Red	Blk	Red	Blk	Gray	Purp	Yell	Yell	Oran
Oran	Blue	Blk	Green	Blk	Blk	Blk	White	Red	Red	Red	Blk
3.3V	-12V	Gnd	P_ON	Gnd	Gnd	Gnd	-5V	5V	5V	5V	Gnd
Pin 13	Pin 14	Pin 15	Pin 16	Pin 17	Pin 18	Pin 19	Pin 20	Pin 21	Pin 22	Pin 23	Pin 24

The color scheme used for each voltage in the 24 pin connector holds for the other ATX standard power supply connectors. However, brand name manufacturers, especially older Dells, often used proprietary power supplies and made up their own color coding, so I wouldn't throw out a power supply that supplies 5V where you think it should supply 3.3V. It's more likely a proprietary design than a failure.

The 5V on Pin 9 is always present when the power supply is plugged in. This connection supplies power to the various PC circuits that operate even when the PC is turned off, such as "Wake on Modem" or "Wake on LAN." It's also the reason you should never work in the PC with the power supply plugged in, unless you can remember to turn off the ATX override switch on the back of the power supply every time. This live power is supplied to the adapter slots, so replacing adapters with the power cord plugged in may damage the motherboard or adapters. Even though the drive leads aren't powered with the system turned off, you might drop a screw while working on a drive. If that screw lands in just the wrong place, like an open bus slot, it could create a short and damage the motherboard.

Live screen?

If your computer has a display connected, can you get a live screen, whether it's a simple text message or a colorful splash screen? If the display shows a message like "No video signal detected," that's the monitor telling you the video port isn't communicating, so you should follow the "No" path for this decision. Sometimes a CRT or older LCD may show a multiplicity of images or endless scrolling, which means the video adapter is alive and trying to transmit an image but the monitor can't interpret the signals. This doesn't happen as often with modern LCDs or expensive CRTs that can match a large range of inputs for higher screen resolutions set in Windows. If you are using a high definition TV for your primary display, do yourself a favor and use a standard monitor for troubleshooting until you eliminate the power supply as an issue.

Newer components like quad core processors and dual PCI Express video adapters have doubled the power requirements of typical gaming PCs. An entry level ATX power supply for a PCI Express gaming PC these days is 600W, and power supplies ranging from 750W to 1000W are no longer unusual. The primary culprits are multi-core CPUs that can consume anywhere from 10W to 50W or more per core, for a total CPU consumption as high as 200W in a single processor system. Meanwhile, PCI Express graphics cards for gaming can pull as much as 200 Watts by themselves, or double that in a dual card configuration.

While PC power supply manufacturers boast about their power rating since it's their main selling point, manufacturers of video cards and other components don't trumpet their power consumption. You may have to do a little math to work it out. Sometimes they give the peak current requirement in Amps (A) at the supply voltage, usually 12V, so you multiply the two numbers for the power consumption in Watts. All of the high end video cards require more power than can be supplied through the PCI Express slot on the motherboard, so they are fed directly from the power supply with one or two 6-pin PCI Express supplementary connectors. Older video adapters employed the 4-pin Molex drive connectors.

A quick search online will help you find a number of calculators for determining your power supply requirement based on the components installed. If the power supply boasts of a peak power rating, don't use that as your guide. Peak power is not sustainable, it's only a meaningful metric for electrical devices with transient demands, like electric car motors that can safely exceed their maximum power rating for short periods during acceleration. PC power demands can remain steady for extended periods, and I like to leave a good 20% margin for error above the computed maximum demand.

If the power comes on but the screen never goes live, try switching back off again and retrying. The switch programming may require you to hold the power button in for a few seconds before the power supply shuts down again. If it refuses to power down, check if there's an override switch on the back of the supply. Otherwise you can turn off your power strip, if you're using one, or just pull the plug. If the PC gets through boot and lights up the screen after a second or third try, it's likely due to miscommunication between the motherboard and power supply around the power_good signal. The power supply is supposed to

delay sending the power_good signal, which tells the CPU it's safe to boot, until the power outputs are stable. This signal allows the CPU to shut itself down if power becomes unstable during regular operation. I've only seen this problem with cheap or failing power supplies, though ironically, some of the cheapest power supplies fake the power_good signal by tying it to their 5V output. If the power_good signal is faked, the computer will try to operate even when power is out of specification, which can easily lead to real data errors before the voltage drops low enough to cause a shutdown.

Beep codes are reported out by the motherboard BIOS diagnostics at power up. A single beep means the POST (Power On Self Test) test was successful and the CPU, memory and video adapter are all reporting present and accounted for. Any longer strings of beeps are usually due to a hardware failure (or something pressing down a key on the keyboard) and the beep codes depend on the manufacturer. Long strings of slow beeps are usually related to a bad memory module, and repeating strings of 3 or 9 beeps often indicate video card failure. In either of these cases, shut down, unplug, and try reseating either the RAM or the video adapter, though it can't hurt to do both. If you are getting beeps with a live screen, the problem is unlikely to be power supply related. Proceed to the Motherboard, CPU and RAM Failure diagnostics.

If you've done any work in the case immediately before the boot failure, undo it, even if it means swapping the old component back in. If a new component prevents the power supply from attaining stability due to excessive current draw, it should cause the power supply to withhold the power_good signal, preventing the motherboard from attempting to boot. The boot failure may be unrelated to the new component, but you could have dislodged a connector, left a loose screw rolling around, or unseated an adapter while working in the case.

A noisy power supply fan can usually be cleaned or replaced easily enough, though you have to watch out for the big capacitors in the power supply when you open it up, even after it's unplugged. Case fans can also fail and make noise, as can the heat sink fans on the CPU, video adapter, or motherboard chipset. And make sure the fan noise isn't due to something stuck in the grille and hitting the fan blades. If your kids hear a whistle that you don't, it's probably beyond your hearing range, and it's not necessarily in the power supply either. I tend to leave these things alone on older PCs if they aren't bothering anybody.

High quality power supplies ship with PWM (Pulse Width Modulation) fans, which are capable of running at much lower RPMs than fans that are controlled by the voltage level. PWM fans require four input leads, ground, 12V, the tachometer output and the PWM control input. Fans with two or three wires can only be controlled by varying the input voltage. PWM fans can typically run down to about a quarter of their rated speed, where voltage controlled fans will usually cease working well before dropping to half of their rated speed. It makes a huge difference in noise output when the higher air circulation, measured in CFM (Cubic Feet per Minute) isn't required.

If you get a text message on the screen that makes any reference to the hard drive, the controller, a SMART error, or any message mentioning the operating system, missing files, etc, proceed to the ATA Drive Failure flowchart. If your power supply is chronically noisy with whistling capacitors or hums, that may be reason enough for you to replace it. And if you've been through the other flowcharts because your PC locks up or reboots at random times, the problem could well be the power supply quality, even if it usually boots the PC.

If you have experience working with a Digital Volt Meter around live voltages, you can try checking the voltages right at the top of the connector to see if they are within reasonable tolerance of the rated voltages. It depends on whether your probe is thin enough and how much room there is next to each wire at the top of the connector to insert the probe. Unfortunately, a simple DVM won't show you whether there is AC ripple on the DC voltages, which can cause all sorts of problems if it's bad enough. An expensive multimeter with sample-and-hold capability and a sampling rate of a few milliseconds can capture the min/max of the DC voltage, showing the presence of ripple without your seeing it as you would on an oscilloscope. This test also requires back-probing the ATX connector or introducing a break-out box between the ATX connector and the motherboard. The test must be performed with the power supply attached to the motherboard for a live load and is only recommended for experienced techs.

Unstable voltages and AC ripple on the DC are real ghosts in the machine, and can mimic all sorts of other problems. If you get into a flaky failure situation that you can't diagnose and you've

HDD or OS error?

Illustrated ATX power supply replacement:

www.fonerbooks.com /r_power.htm

already started swapping parts, you may as well try a new power supply as well. I've seen power supplies produce some really bizarre failures, like a PC that reboots when you set your coffee cup down too hard on the table. The most pervasive of the unstable power supply problems are random lockups or spontaneous reboots. Modern motherboards have some ability to regulate the power they receive, but it's got to be within a reasonable range, and the power supply has to cooperate by monitoring its own output and reporting through the power_good signal.

Forced hard drive spin up?

We've reached this point because there was no sign of the PC powering on at the beginning of the flowchart. Unless you have an SSD boot drive, you should also hear a very subdued clicking or chuckling from the arm with the read/write head moving in and out. Take the side off the PC case and make sure there are no signs of life, that none of fans in the case are spinning, including the CPU fan, the video adapter fan and any case fans.

Next, unplug the power supply from the wall, and then disconnect all of the power supply leads from the motherboard, the video adapter, any auxiliary fans, the DVD. The only component that should be connected to the power supply when you're done is the hard drive. If there's more than one hard drive installed, you can leave those power leads connected as well. If the power supply is from a quality manufacturer, you should be able to determine the minimum load required for it to turn on, and a standard hard drive is normally sufficient. A quality power supply without a sufficient load will refuse to turn on (shutting itself off quickly) even when forced, but a cheap power supply may damage itself.

If you're competent to work around live DC voltages in an open case, try to force the power supply on by shorting the green wire (pin 16, power_on) to any of the black wires (grounds) in the main ATX motherboard power connector, which is either 20 or 24 pins. The power supply may instantly turn itself off again if there if there is a short circuit in the hard drive or if the load is insufficient. If the power supply comes on and the hard drive spins up, the power supply is probably good.

If the power doesn't come on, double check that the power lead is firmly seated in the drive socket. Old style Molex connectors used on old IDE hard drives were notoriously hard to insert in the socket, and they rarely ever seated all the way. Try switching to a different power supply lead, and if there are multiple hard drives connected, try each one in turn.

The previous test only gives a decisive result if you performed it with a proven good hard drive. You can either test your existing hard drive in another PC or in an external USB case attached to a laptop, or you can obtain a known good working hard drive from another PC. The capacity, speed, etc, of the hard drive is irrelevant to the test. Any working hard drive with the right connector for the power supply will do. However, if you ever thought there was a burnt smell or sparks coming from the drive area in your PC or from the drive itself, don't test it in a good PC, or you risk causing damage if it failed as a short circuit.

If you can't get power to come on and the hard drive to spin up when bypassing the motherboard and forcing power on, either the ATX power supply has failed or the hard drive does not present a sufficient electrical load for the switching power supply to operate. And if you live in a region with irregular power from the utility or if you are operating off-the-grid with home generated power, you should make sure the supply voltage is in the acceptable range for the power supply, which does require a volt meter.

If you're working on a server that uses SCSI drives, make sure the SCSI jumper to delay drive spin-up isn't set. This used to be necessary in SCSI drive arrays so they wouldn't all spin up at once and swamp the power supply. The default is usually for the SCSI adapter to spin them up following their SCSI ID sequence.

Since the PC powered up with nothing but the hard drive connected, the power supply is probably good and there is either an excessive current draw or a short somewhere on the motherboard or the other attached components. With the power supply unplugged, reconnect all of the power leads you removed in the previous step, then try powering up again just to make sure a bad connection wasn't your problem all along.
If this doesn't work, you'll now have to locate the problem component through the process of elimination.

Start by removing the power and data cables from the DVD drive, you can do this with the power supply plugged in. If the system doesn't start, the DVD isn't the problem, so the next step is to start removing adapters, one at a time, leaving the video for last. Unplug the power cord or switch off the power strip before removing each adapter, then reconnect to power up. If the

system powers up, replace all adapters except the last one removed before power came on. If power still comes on, try the last adapter you removed in different slot before giving up on it. If you find an adapter that actually prevents the system from powering up, it must be replaced. If you are running with dual PCI Express video cards, try running with just one and then just the other. If you have a single high speed video card slot, whether PCI Express or the older AGP technology, it could be that slot is faulty. Another possibility if you're using parts from older PCs that date back to the last technology transition is that the adapter is keyed as universal but is installed on a new motherboard that expects low voltage AGP adapters (AGP 4X or 8X).

In rare instances, the motherboard circuitry for the power switch may have been damaged. If you can see the conductors through the top of the main ATX connector, you can try shorting green to black again with the connector still on the motherboard. If power comes on, shut down again and reinstall the other components. If forcing the power on works again, one possible work-around is to rig the front panel power switch direct to the connector power_on and ground. I don't recommend permanently shorting the two pins because you'll never be able to shut down from Windows (the system will simply restart) and because the power_on circuit is intended for momentary switching action, not to be tied to ground.

Once you've eliminated the drives and the adapters, one of the few remaining possibilities is a motherboard short. Remove the motherboard and check for a standoff or screw installed in the wrong place or rolling around loose. I often build out systems on the bench without a case, supporting the motherboard on a static proof bag over a cardboard box or some similar arrangement to give the adapters room to seat. This method eliminates any case mounting issues from the troubleshooting process, but it introduces all sorts of risks, not the least of which is absence of the case ground.

Normally, a short circuit will result in a burnt smell and a ruined motherboard, sometimes damaging any of the attached components (memory, CPU, adapters) as well. In many instances, you'll be able to figure out which component is ruined by the presence of burn marks or a strong odor of smoke coming from the component, though when it happens in a closed case, the smoky smell can stick to everything. If you can't locate a failed component by visual inspection, you need to have access to a test-bed system (an inexpensive but completely functioning PC for testing questionable parts). Don't test parts that may be fried in a good system, because some types of failures will cause damage to the next machine.

If you've reached this point without ever getting the system to power up, you probably have a defective motherboard. Because power isn't coming on at all with the motherboard attached, it's very unlikely that the problem is the power supply failing to produce all of the different voltages required by the motherboard. It is possible that the power supply circuit for sensing over-current conditions has failed in such a way that it is refusing to power up with a motherboard that would work with a different power supply.

I always try swapping the power supply as a final test because it's easy to pull a spare out of another system, and with the motherboard on the bench, you can usually make the leads reach without even taking the known good power supply out of the donor PC. Repairing power supplies requires a good knowledge of electronics as there are usually "no user serviceable parts." Even when power supplies are unplugged, they can give nasty zap from stored power in the electrolytic capacitors.

Video Failure

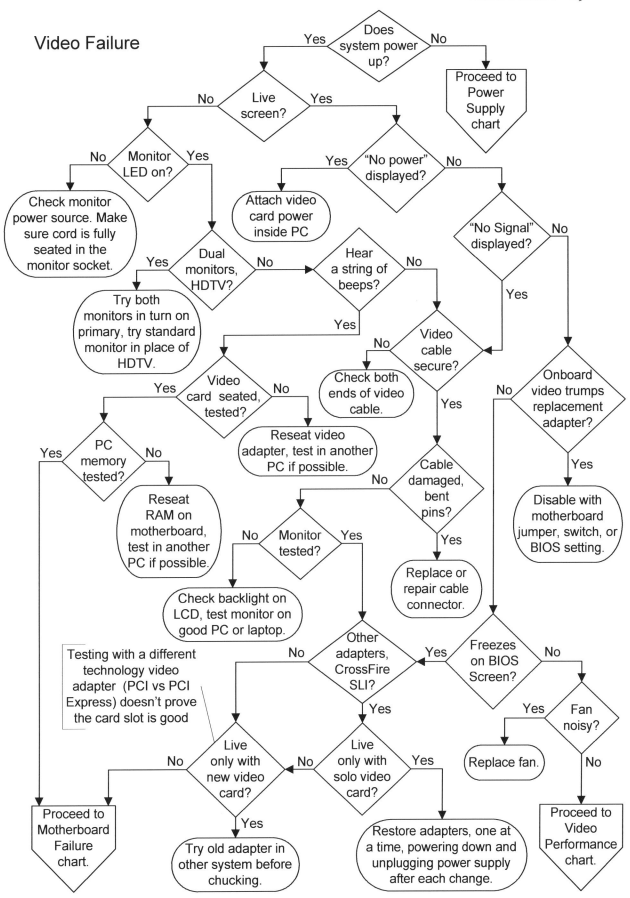

Video Failure

Is the system power coming on? Can you hear fans turning and drive motors spinning up, see little lights on the front of the CPU case, hear any beeps? We're talking about system power here, not the monitor power. If the system isn't powering up, or if you aren't sure whether or not it is, go to the Power Supply Failure chart now.

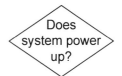

Do you see anything on the screen of your LCD or CRT (Cathode Ray Tube) monitor? This doesn't have to be your Windows desktop appearing. Text or scrolling messages count for "anything" in this step. The next few steps along either path determine if there is a simple problem with power or connections for the monitor or video adapter.

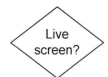

Are you sure the monitor is powered and turned on? Don't laugh. All modern monitors have some form of status light, usually right next to or inside the power button, to tell you when they are powered on. Even old CRT monitors usually have a status LED that lights up when the monitor is powered and may blink or change color depending on whether there's an active video card detected. Large CRTs generally make a noise when they power on, a combination of static cling and something like a rubber band being strummed once. Both types of monitors, LCDs and CRTs, normally utilize a detachable power cord, so make sure the male end is fully seated in the monitor's power port. If you still aren't getting any signs of life from the monitor, try a different power outlet.

You may encounter an old LCD display with an external power supply, similar to the AC adapter for charging a laptop battery. If you have such an old LCD and it's not powering up, use a multimeter to check that DC output from the AC/DC adapter is approximately the same as the faceplate rating. In all cases, LCD displays are designed to take up the minimum of desktop space, so they tend to have the power cord plug in vertically, in parallel with the LCD screen on the back, rather than on the perpendicular. That makes it hard to inspect the connection unless you lay the screen flat or hold it above your head, so just make sure the cord is in as far as it goes.

Multiple monitor setups are becoming increasingly popular with power users who either want to increase the size of their desktop for a larger work area, or display different windows on different screens. In multiple monitor setups, one of the video outputs is the primary. This is true whether you have multiple video outputs from a single graphics adapter or multiple video cards as well. When troubleshooting a "no live screen" situation, concentrate on getting the primary monitor, the one that's active during the boot process, up and running. Try each monitor in turn on the primary video output, as the odds of two monitors dying at the same time is low.

If you are using an HDTV as the primary monitor, and especially if this is a new build or if you've just upgraded your PC, try to get live with a standard monitor first if you have one available. HDTVs don't always do a perfect job emulating computer monitors, it's not their main design goal. Simply getting an HDTV to work properly on a new video adapter sometimes requires updates from nVidia, AMD or Intel, changing settings choices on the HDTV with the remote control, or a new HDMI cable. If the PC doesn't automatically detect the screen resolution and refresh rate the HDTV is capable of displaying, you may need to connect a regular monitor just to choose a better match in Windows screen settings. Check the maximum refresh rate allowed by the HDTV before proceeding because it's possible that overdriving it could damage the television. I've heard horror stories about losing the HDTV display after upgrading Windows versions. A solution depends on the availability of updated drivers and sometimes an updated BIOS.

If the only message your monitor displays is something that includes the word "power," it's probably informing you that the video adapter in the PC requires additional power to operate. The video card is alive, it's generating the message, but the motherboard slot doesn't supply enough power for it to function normally. Both the current crop of PCI Express cards and the higher performance AGP graphics cards that preceded PCI Express usually require one or more dedicated leads from the power supply. If you've just built the PC, it means you forgot to connect the power supply lead or didn't make the connection properly. If it's a PC you just had open for a different reason, you probably loosened the power cord connection enough to break the circuit. But if the case hasn't been open since the last time you booted successfully, it's likely the power supply circuit has failed or there's a hardware failure on the video card.

These supplementary power leads come in many forms, from the old fashioned 4x1 Molex connectors used in PCs since the 1980's, to the dedicated PCI Express video power connectors on the latest ATX power supplies. Some video cards will accept multiple types of power leads since it's just a little extra real estate on the card, but others will force you to find an adapter to convert from an available connector to one the video card will accept. When a power supply offers an 8-pin PCI Express connector and your video card requires 6-pin, you can buy an inexpensive 8-pin to 6-pin (or 6+2 pin) adapter, or you can modify the cable connector in accordance with instructions on the graphics card manufacturer's website.

Most new monitors will display a text message like "No signal source," or "Attach video signal," as long as they are healthy, and powered on. These messages should appear even if the PC or video adapter is dead. This is actually one of the more useful innovations in monitor technology, because it offers definitive proof that the monitor or LCD display is alive and most likely capable of displaying an image if a video signal was present. Unfortunately, the message only proves something if it appears, since older monitors and cheaper models may not display anything at all, and some video adapter or boot failures may result in the display of a black (blank) screen.

Today there are several different video cables in wide use, depending on the generation of technology. The oldest of these supports up to 15 conductors (3 rows of 5 pins each in the connector) for analog video signals, and has been in use since the early 1990's. The modern DVI (Digital Video Interface) cables come in several varieties, with up to 24 contacts for digital transmission and an optional 5 contacts to support older analog signals. The HDMI (High Definition Multimedia Interface) uses 19 or 29 conductors in one of five connector types which support miniature video devices and cameras as well as displays. HDMI is backwards compatible to DVI, so you can buy HDMI to DVI or DVI to HDMI adapters.

Whatever technology you are using, the connector must be seated squarely on (or in) the video port on the back of the system. The hold-down screws on either side of the connectors that have them should be screwed in all the way, but not made up too tight. The same is true for the connector on the monitor or HDTV end of the cable. If you have recently moved the system or changed any components which required you to undo one of the connections, remove that end and inspect the connector and port for damage.

Do you hear a string of beeps? Healthy PCs should only beep once when they are turned on and pass their Power On Self Test (POST) routine. While different BIOS manufacturers use different beep codes to identify failures, a repeating string of beeps (three or nine in a row) is a common indicator of video card failure. But don't be tricked by an unending stream of beeps which can be caused by something leaning on the keyboard and holding down a key at boot.

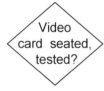

Check whether or not the video adapter is properly seated, but first unplug the power supply before removing any adapter installed on the motherboard. If you have more than one video adapter installed, remove the secondary video adapter, and if you still don't get a live screen, swap the secondary for the primary. Likewise, if you have an add-in video adapter installed as a performance upgrade to built-in motherboard video, remove it and try getting a live screen with the built-in GPU, even if this means changing a jumper or switch on the motherboard to re-enable it.

When reseating a video adapter, always remove it completely from the slot, making sure to release the hold-down latch if it exists, then reseat the adapter by pushing down evenly at the front and back on the top edge. Be careful that installing a hold-down screw or hold down rail for adapters at the back of the case doesn't lever the front (towards the front of the PC) end of the video adapter up a fraction of an inch out of the slot, because that's all it takes if there's no hold-down latch. And don't forget to redo the hold-down latch once the card is seated.

If reseating the card doesn't clear up the beeps, it's probably a failed video adapter or bad RAM on the motherboard. You can power down and try reseating the RAM at this point, without going all the way through the motherboard diagnostics. There used to be beep codes for all sorts of component failures, but most of those components have long since been integrated into the motherboard chipset and can't be replaced if they fail.

If reseating the PC memory on the motherboard doesn't clear up the problem, you can further troubleshoot the possibility that the system RAM is the problem by testing it in another PC or by running with the minimum number of modules. Depending on the motherboard and the type of DIMM installed (single sided, double sided), the PC may have multiple DIMMS installed and only require a single DIMM in Bank 0 for boot. DIMM sockets are labeled with text printed on the motherboard or color coded to show the banks.

Motherboards with multiple banks operating in dual channel or triple channel mode require a handful of exactly matched DIMMs if fully populated. In the "ganged" designs, the availability of two 64 bit memory modules on a single bus means a single processor has access to a 128 bit wide memory bus. In current "unganged" implementations, multi-core (and multi-threading) processors can address 64 bit wide memory at the same time, a way of adding a second memory bus to the system.

Examine the full length of the video cable for evidence of a sharp indentation in the outer sheathing, which would indicate the cable was pinched and may be damaged. Male video connectors are all subject to pin damage, although the HDMI designs deploy the pins as edge connectors, so it's pretty hard to injure them unless you stick a screwdriver in the connector and twist it. DVI connector pins are beefier than the older analog VGA connector pins, and the analog compatibility section on one end of the DVI connector makes it nearly impossible to get confused and try to force the connector on the wrong way. It's the attempts to force a VGA connector on the wrong way while working blindly behind a monitor or PC that generally cause pin damage.

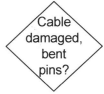

Carefully examine the pins to make sure none of them are at an angle, touching other pins, or flattened against the bottom of the connector. Note that missing pins in a video cable are the norm, often the monitor ID pins or other signals not used by the monitor with which the cable shipped. It's nice if you have a spare video cable and a monitor with a detachable cable to swap, but older CRTs often used a cable that wasn't detachable on the monitor end. You'll have to settle for visual inspection for whether such a cable may have been crushed or breached.

If you see that a pin in the connector is bent, you can try to straighten it very slowly with tweezers or fine needle nose pliers. If a pin breaks, you can buy a replacement connector and solder it on with a fine soldering iron and infinite patience. You'll also need a heat shrink gun and tubing if you want to do it right. The last time I did one it took me almost three hours, though I didn't have the right soldering iron tip to work between three rows of pins. I don't recommend making your own DVI connector.

Before making yourself nuts, test the monitor on another PC or laptop. If you use a laptop to test the monitor and it doesn't automatically detect an external monitor when booting, use the "Fn" function keys along the top of the keyboard to tell the laptop to shift to the external display. Remember that we are testing just to see if the monitor is live, it doesn't matter if the screen settings are wrong and the display looks funny. If the monitor doesn't work on a known good computer, the problem is with the monitor, not your PC. If a faint image is detectable on an LCD screen when you shine a bright light at it on an angle, the problem is with the backlight or the inverter that powers the backlight. A loud buzz coming from an LCD monitor is often the inverter circuit failing, though it can go on getting louder for years before it pops.

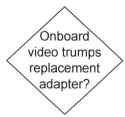

Do you keep seeing the GPU (Graphics Processor Unit) from the motherboard announcing itself when the PC powers on, even though you've replaced it with an add-in video adapter, whether PCI Express, or an older AGP or plain PCI adapter? You need to disable the onboard GPU, either by changing the video setting in CMOS Setup, or with a jumper or dip switch on the motherboard. Sometimes, the on-board GPU will be set to "On" or "Enabled" in CMOS, when you need it to be "Off" or "Disabled." If it is set to "Auto" for automatic or autodetect, that setting obviously isn't working so change it to "Off" or "Disabled."

Does the system get as far as showing the BIOS screen and then locking up? By BIOS screen, we're talking about the text information or brand-name graphics that appear on the screen in the initial boot stages from the video adapter or motherboard. A system that freezes up at this point is rarely suffering from a video failure, though a conflict between the video card and another installed adapter is still possible.

Is a heatsink fan on the video adapter or on a motherboard integrated GPU noisy, or worse, not functioning? If the video heatsink fan is healthy and you have reached this point in the diagnostics, it's likely your problem is related to video performance rather than out-and-out failure, so proceed to the Video Performance flowchart.

A modern GPU without active cooling will soon fail, and one symptom is slow performance as the GPU warms up and throttles its own performance to try to reduce heat generation. Some GPU fans are replaceable if you can find the right size, you'll usually need a millimeter ruler to determine the screw spacing. In other cases, you may need to replace the entire active heatsink, which presents two challenges. First, you'll have to find a replacement that fits, and second, you'll have to detach the old heatsink from the GPU, where it is often attached by a heat conductive adhesive.

If there's no spring clip or screws holding the heatsink in place, all you can do is wait until the graphics card is cold since the adhesive will be less tacky (some people bag and freeze the video adapter first) and try to wedge in a bit of stiff, thin plastic in from the edge. Unless the adhesive is failing, you'll probably need to pry at the edge of the heatsink with a screwdriver while trying to slide the plastic (a supermarket card works well) further in, both to slice through the adhesive and to keep up the pressure to separate. If the GPU breaks while you're prying, don't be surprised.

Are you running a dual adapter setup for increased video performance, such as nVidia SLI or AMD CrossFire? Unplug the power supply and try removing one of the adapters before powering up again. Note that older motherboards designed for SLI and CrossFire may have shipped with a "PCIe switch" or "PCIe terminator" which was installed in the second x16 slot if only one video adapter was used, allowing the single adapter to utilize the full x16 lanes. If the screen remains frozen or dark at boot, try swapping it with the other adapter. Both AMD and nVidia offer interactive troubleshooting databases for their high performance video adapters through their websites.

Did you install any new adapters immediately before the problem appeared? With the power disconnected, remove any other adapters, one at a time, then reconnect power and attempt to reboot after each removal. Locking up on the BIOS screen is often due to an adapter conflict, but if removing the other adapters doesn't solve the problem, proceed to Motherboard, CPU and RAM Failure.

Do you only get a live screen, or at least move past the BIOS screen, when all the other adapters are removed? If so, the problem is either a bad adapter preventing proper operation of the bus or an adapter conflicting with the video card. In either case, you can reinstall the adapters one at a time, powering up after each one, troubleshooting the problem by process of elimination. Don't forget to unplug the system each time before taking any action inside the case.

One reason for a video adapter to not work is if it isn't compatible with the motherboard. If you have an older motherboard, it could be that your x16 PCIe 3.0 or even PCIe 2.1 adapter isn't actually supported by the motherboard slot. PCI Express cards are generally backwards compatible, although they transfer data slower over the same number of lanes, but it's easy to fall into the trap of thinking they are always backwards compatible. Some PCIe adapters (2.1) are not backwards compatible all the way to 1.0 unless the motherboard maker has released a BIOS update that addresses chipset settings.

If the motherboard is a new upgrade, try the "failed" video adapter in another system before trashing it, since it could be a simple incompatibility. If installing a new video adapter doesn't solve your "dead screen" problem, it's likely a motherboard failure issue, even though you got to this point without any beep codes. Proceed to Motherboard, CPU and RAM Failure.

Video
Monitor and
Adapter
Performance

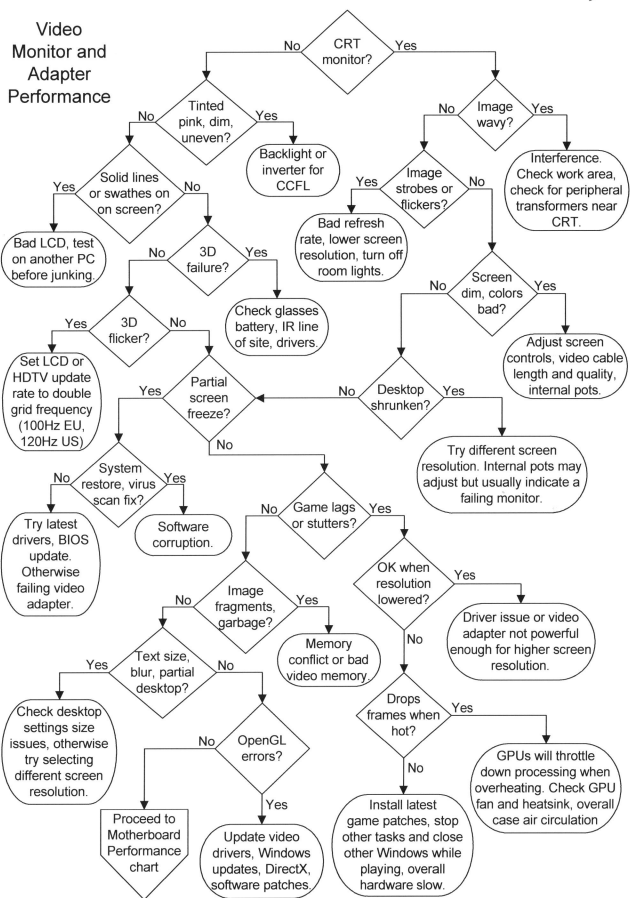

Video Performance

Is the display monitor a CRT (Cathode Ray Tube)? Some CRT monitors are still in use, especially larger, high performance models that people paid a lot of money for and which have some advantages over the various flat panel technologies. The CRT technology, which employs high voltages and high frequency waveforms (analog) to selectively paint colored dots of phosphorus on the display surface of the glass tube with an electron beam, is subject to a different set of performance issues than the digital LCD technology.

Is the image wavy, contorting in a regular manner, or is there scan line interference? The most common source of a wavy CRT image is magnetic interference, usually from a small transformer located right below or above the monitor, like the power supply for an inkjet or other peripheral device. Other image distortions and scan lines can be due to an active RF source, like a radio transmitter, or heavy duty currents flowing in nearby wall wiring.

If eliminating nearby sources of possible interference or temporarily relocating the monitor to another room as a test doesn't clear up the problem, it's likely the failure of a discrete part in the electronic control circuitry that can be located and replaced by an experienced CRT technician. Of course, you should test the monitor on another PC before taking it for repair. Another remote possibility is bad power regulation. If your power is supplied by a windmill from the early generations of wind power in an off-the-grid area, like a large island, check that the utility (or private) power source isn't straying off the basic 60 Hz (US) or 50Hz (EU) base AC power frequency.

Do you have the feeling that somebody is trying to sell you something through subliminal advertising? Try looking at the screen out of the corner of your eye or from across the room, because peripheral vision is more sensitive to rapid movements against a still background. The most common reason for a flickering display is that the horizontal refresh rate is too slow or is caught in a cyclical pattern with fluorescent room lighting.

First thing, try extinguishing all electrical lights in the room and see if the flicker clears up. If it does, and if you don't want to change your screen resolution, you can try changing the lighting or the location of the monitor in relation to the room lighting. Second, try lowering your screen resolution in Windows. The higher the screen resolution, the harder it is for the video adapter and the monitor to support a high vertical refresh rate, and it's not unusual for older video adapters to drop the rate to 60 Hz when the resolution is at maximum.

Because the input to CRT monitors is an analog RGB (Red, Green, Blue) signal, the condition of the cable and the cable length matters to the appearance of the image. Digital is generally a pass/fail technology, while analog can limp by with low quality inputs, but the quality of the image will suffer. Six feet is about as long as you want to go with an old analog video cable, through plenty of vendors are happy to sell extensions or longer replacement cables that perform with mixed results. When you crank up the brightness on your CRT to compensate for a longer cable, don't be surprised if you start to hear a whistling capacitor or transformer hum as the monitor is overworked. If the video cable has been pinched in a drawer or behind a desk, etc, it's possible to lose one of the primary colors without seeing any damage to the connectors.

CRT monitors are tuned at the factory for brightness, contrast, hue, color balance, everything you can think of relating to a color image. Newer monitors may allow the technician to make all of the adjustments through the user controls, but the analog circuitry inside of the monitors typically includes adjustable pots for fine tuning. These adjustments can only be made with a plastic (nonconducting) screwdriver, and are only recommended for experienced technicians, as they must be made with a live flyback transformer putting out over ten thousand volts. If you've lost a primary color completely, even when you move the monitor to another system to eliminate the possibility that the video card has blown a D/A converter channel, it usually means you have lost one of the three color guns within the CRT tube, and the monitor isn't worth repairing.

If your Windows desktop doesn't extend out to the edges of the monitor, you can use the controls on the front of the monitor to try to compensate. It's not unusual for the desktop to change size or to shift a little towards one of the edges when you change the screen resolution in Windows with older video adapter/CRT combinations. And if the controls don't get the desktop back to the center of the screen and extended out to the edges, you should try changing the Windows screen resolution again. You will occasionally encounter an old monitor where the image has shrunk, usually asymmetrically, and you can't get it back to normal using the screen controls. As described above, an experienced technician may be able to restore the desktop symmetry by adjusting the internal pots with a nonconductive screwdriver, but it's a sure sign of a failing monitor.

Is the image correct, except the color is tinted pink, or unevenly lit? If you are using an OLED (Organic LED) monitor, skip this decision point. Think of the LCD as a sort of electronic color film. If you remember the old 35 mm slides that used to be popular in photography, you'll remember how hard it was to make out the picture without a slide projector or a light table. The light source that turns the LCD "film" into a bright display is called the "backlight." LCDs can use either a CCFL (Cold Cathode Fluorescent Lamp) tube backlight or a string of LEDs. Both the CCFL tubes and the LEDs are relatively long lived, but CCFL tubes require a special power source to light them, an inverter. The power is provided by the inverter, which creates a high voltage, high frequency electronic signal.

If the LCD only displays the faintest of images, only detectable if you shine a bright light at it on an angle, it means the backlight isn't lit. If the whole screen is tinted pink, you probably have a failing CCFL tube. If the screen is darker at one or the other edges, it could be a failing tube or inverter, or a bad LED if you have an LED strip backlight. Dimness towards the center of the screen would likely be a bad LED backlight. The power supply for LED backlights is rarely the culprit because it supplies straight DC for full brightness and chopped DC for dimming.

LCD screens are subject to matrix addressing failures that aren't an issue with CRT monitors. LCD manufacturers usually have a standard for the number of dead or stuck pixels that must appear on a display before they will accept that it is defective for warranty return. There are over a million individual pixels on the typical LCD, but a single failed pixel in the middle of the viewing area can drive some people nuts. Don't forget to make sure it isn't just a spot of dust.

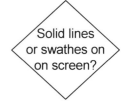

When an entire line of pixels fails, either horizontally or vertically, or when a large fraction of the display goes dead from end to end, it means that either the bonding of the electrical contacts to the LCD have failed or one of the multiplexer chips that address the LCD grid (or a single output line on the chip) is dead. These aren't home repairs, and other than factory warranty repairs, they generally aren't worth doing since it normally means replacing the entire LCD panel or the whole circuit board.

If a random sized blob or growing plume shows up on your LCD and it's not a foreign substance stuck to the screen, it means the bonding of the layers in the LCD panel have failed and the liquid is leaking. This will generally only happen if the screen has been cracked or impacted with a sharp object, so the LCD manufacturer will likely try to claim that you caused the damage, even if it's within warranty.

Are 3D games and applications failing to appear as 3D? Almost all video games employ 3D images, in the sense of using perspective to create a false illusion of depth, but true stereoscopic 3D is only supported by some games and applications. Stereoscopic 3D works by presenting different images to the right and left eyes, which the brain puts together to create an image that appears to extend beyond the confines of the screen.

Monitors and HDTVs that support stereoscopic 3D are usually advertised as "3D ready." The main figure of merit is that they will support a refresh rate of 120 Hz, which allows them to present alternating images for the right and left eye at a rate of 60Hz. The first step is to make sure that your monitor is 3D ready, your game is a 3D game, and all of the proper software drivers are installed in Windows for the 3D capable video adapter. Any additional software required by the game, such as the latest version of DirectX, must be updated, patched and installed. Make sure you are using a dual DVI cable for high resolution 3D if required (it should ship with your 3D ready monitor), and make sure that the game appears in the 3D compatibility list of the video adapter maker.

If you have a newer technology display that uses passive 3D glasses (no battery), skip this step. If you still aren't seeing 3D images, the problem is likely with the 3D glasses or the IR (Infra Red) emitter that communicates with the glasses. If you have wired glasses (tethered to a USB port), you don't need an IR emitter or battery, so you can skip this paragraph. The most common problem is something obstructing the line of sight between the IR emitter and the glasses, which could be anything from a cup of coffee to something on your computer table. The next possibility is that the battery in the 3D glasses is dead and needs to be recharged, see the instructions for your particular glasses. Check also that the IR emitter is plugged in and the status LED (if it has one) is lit.

Do you see 3D but it flickers? As long as you are using a 3D ready monitor, video card and cable, it's unlikely that the flicker is due to the refresh being too slow. You are probably seeing a strobe effect from artificial lighting in the room because the monitor refresh rate isn't matched to the lighting. Think of it like the old Western movies where the wagon wheels would appear to move backwards at some point because the camera frame rate was catching the wheel spokes at a relatively slow sample rate. In the US and other 60 Hz distribution countries, you should make sure the monitor is set to 120 Hz, where as in the EU and 50 Hz distribution countries, you should set the monitor for a 100 Hz refresh. Use 110 Hz in natural lighting.

If changing the refresh rate doesn't help, try turning off the artificial room lighting. Make sure that you have chosen a Windows screen resolution that is supported by the monitor. Some of the new HDTVs display 3D using passive glasses (just colored lenses, no battery or IR emitter), and if you have one of these, the only remaining option is to try adjusting the software settings to see if the problem is really video card performance. The 3D depth should be adjustable in the graphics adapter control software, and it's recommended that people new to 3D gaming start at a depth of 15%, to get used to 3D effects. 3D display drivers and adapters are generally designed for 1080i (a 1920 by 1080 screen resolution) so 3D will fail or flicker badly if you try to run the game in a window, rather than full screen. Note also that some LCD monitors actually require a brief warm up period (15 – 30 minutes) for the CCFL backlight to reach full brightness, which is critical for 3D.

Does a part of your desktop freeze-up while you are still able to work in other windows or sections of the screen? We're talking about entire windows freezing here, not stuck pixels, mouse tracks, or lines. In some cases, the frozen section may refresh if you end the task in Windows Task Manager.

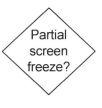

My favorite trick for dealing with possible system software errors in recent years is to run Windows System Restore. Just choose a restore date from before the problem appeared, and if the problem is due to a corrupted software setting or a simple virus, it should be fixed. The working assumption here is that everybody is running virus and malware protection, but even if

you are, the next step is to download a free malware checker (don't trust Google search here, see your favorite computer publication for reviews so you don't end up installing evil software) and make sure nothing new slipped past your protection.

If that doesn't fix the problem, try installing any updated drivers and patches for the video adapter, which may include a BIOS update. After that, the likely culprit is the video memory, but you shouldn't see this problem unless the memory is failing or it's getting way too hot inside the case, so check that your case fans are drawing cooling air into the case and exhausting it at the back. If you have both an add-in video adapter and a less powerful GPU integrated on the motherboard, it's a good time to enable the motherboard video, remove the add-in video card, and see if the freezing windows clear up. Check the heatsink fan on the GPU, whether it's on an add-in card, a separate chip on the motherboard, or integrated with a newer high performance CPU, to make sure that it's working.

Does the action in your game seem to slow down, and then catch up again in a burst, or are frames getting dropped so you feel like you are looking at the screen through a rotating ceiling fan? Playing games demands much more performance from the PC than the vast majority of applications because the action must happen in real-time, so gaming is seen as the true test of graphics system performance. The most processing intensive tasks of modern games fall upon the GPU which handles the rendering, but keep in mind that many PC components, including the motherboard, CPU, memory, and hard drive, are also being pushed to their limits by gaming.

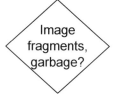

If you see little fragments of letters, little colored bits of screen, a few pixels here and there that stay the wrong color until you reboot the PC, it's probably the GPU or video memory failing. If you have an integrated GPU on the motherboard (you can tell if the video connector is located near the edge of the case along with the USB ports, network port, etc, as opposed to in one of the cut-out slots for add in cards), the video memory is usually borrowed from the main PC memory, and some newer CPUs from both AMD and Intel include a GPU on the same chip.

If the video is integrated with the motherboard, swapping the memory is the only way to determine if it is the source of the problem. If you have an add-in video adapter, you'll have to try a replacement. Random garbage that appears momentarily and then clears up can be due to the graphics card switching modes, especially when launching games or switching applications. If you're watching TV, make sure closed captioning isn't turned on and unsupported, as in a foreign language.

Is screen text blurry, the text size wrong, or do you have to scroll to see the entire area of the Windows desktop? The first step is to try changing the basic Windows options for the screen appearance. These settings get different names in different versions of Windows, but you can generally access them by right-clicking in an empty area of the Desktop and choosing "Properties" to see the options. Note that you want the Windows properties here, not the properties for the graphics adapter, which may appear in the same drop-down list that results from right-clicking.

Text size, blur, partial desktop?

If selecting a different font size or different visual properties doesn't help, it probably means that the graphics adapter properties are set to a screen resolution in Windows that isn't supported by the monitor. These settings may appear both under Windows properties for the display (a Windows setting) and under the graphics properties for the adapter. Don't assume that you need to choose a lower screen resolution here. Blurry text is normally the result of trying to display too low of a resolution on an LCD screen.

Are you getting error messages on the screen referring to OpenGL? Open Graphics Library (OpenGL) is a widely used standard programming interface that is used to call for hardware acceleration of graphics rendering tasks. OpenGL errors are more common on older Windows operating systems (Windows XP and older), and solutions range from installing the latest video drivers to choosing "High Color" (16 bit color) on the Windows Desktop and closing all other windows. And make sure you don't have "hardware acceleration" turned off under the display adapter properties. If you record the specific error and post a question to the support forum of the GPU maker, along with all the pertinent information like your operating system version, graphics card, the game or application you are running, CPU, etc, you may get an answer.

OpenGL errors?

If you are running CrossFire or SLI paired graphics adapters and aren't seeing the speed you expected, make sure the motherboard is approved by the vendor (AMD or Intel) and that the two graphics adapters are identical, running the same clock speed. The faster adapter will slow down to match the lower clock. Otherwise, it's possible that your video performance issue is really a PC performance issue, so it's worth going through the flowchart for motherboard, CPU and RAM performance troubleshooting.

Does the degree of stutter or performance lag change with the screen resolution, the density of detail in a given area? Make sure you have downloaded the latest driver and patches from the GPU manufacturer's website. If the game uses DirectX, it's a good time to make sure you have downloaded the latest version of DirectX from Microsoft as well. If the game maker suggests a particular screen resolution and set of display parameters to run the game, make sure you are using them.

Of course, lower resolution (less detail in the screen area) means less processing, so you may just have a bottleneck in the system. Try closing all other windows, manually shutting down Windows tasks if necessary, and see if the video smoothes out. If so, the GPU is probably fine, and the problem either lies with the performance of other PC components or you are simply asking the PC to do too much at the same time. Advanced users may want to try disabling their virus software, though if you are connected to the Internet for multi-user gaming, this isn't a good idea unless you've studied up on firewalls.

If you've shut down all the tasks you possibly can without crashing the operating system, and the game performance still improves at a lower screen resolution, it's probable that your GPU just can't do any better. This is to be expected if you have a low cost motherboard with an integrated GPU, but it is less probable if you've purchased an expensive add-in graphics card or if you have one of the newer multi-core CPUs with a powerful GPU integrated in the same package.

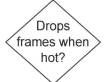

Does the game drop frames (skip forward) when the PC heats up? To protect itself from overheating without forcing a total shutdown, the GPU may intentionally throttle back when it starts to overheat. But the implication is still that the GPU is not being cooled properly, which could be due to a number of different reasons. The first thing to check is that the fan on the GPU hasn't failed. Next, make sure that the whole PC isn't overheating by checking that the intake vents haven't been blocked and cool air is being drawn into the case, as well as getting exhausted out the back. It's also important to pay attention to the temperature in the room. The PC is dependent on the ambient air for cooling, so the warmer the room, the less cooling the PC will generate from circulating the air through the case.

If the issue isn't heat related, you're back to making sure that you have every possible software patch and driver upgrade installed, shutting down background tasks to make sure you aren't dealing with an overall PC performance issue, and communicating with other people in the game maker's forum to see if anybody is seeing the same kind of performance issues as you are. If you have a PCIe SSD drive installed in a high speed PCI Express slot, it's possible your PCIe x16 video adapter is dropping to x8 because the SSD x16 drive is sharing available bandwidth.

Double check that the version of the PCIe motherboard slots (1.1, 2.1, 3.0), is greater than or equal to the PCIe version of your video adapter, or the motherboard could be the bottleneck. Also make sure you are running x16 video adapters in true x16 slots, not compatibility mode slots labeled x16 (x8) or the like. If a number of people with the same type of hardware or similar software installed are seeing the same performance issues, there may be a basic compatibility problem.

Motherboard, CPU, RAM Failure

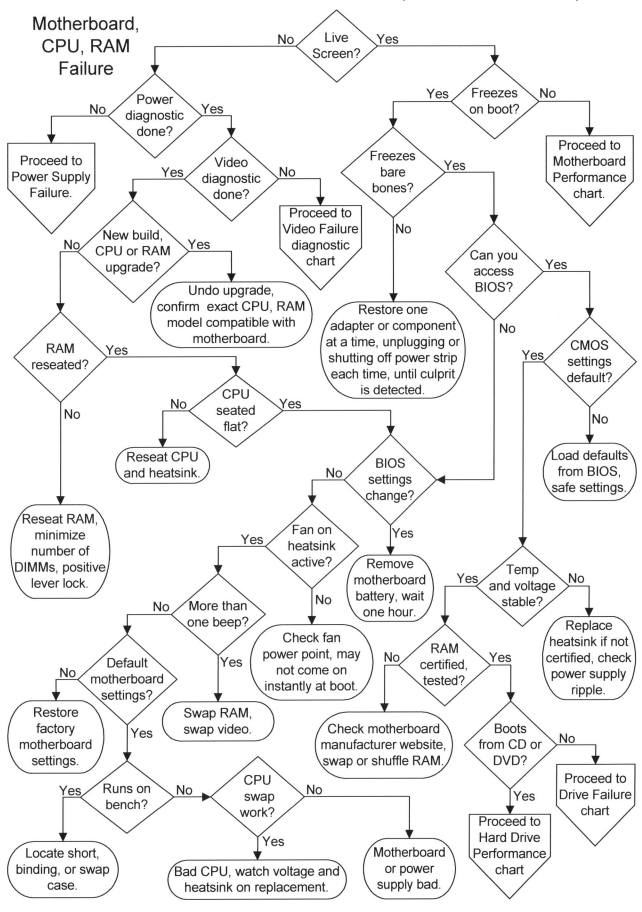

Live Screen?
- No →
- Yes →

Power diagnostic done?
- No → Proceed to Power Supply Failure.
- Yes →

Video diagnostic done?
- Yes →
- No → Proceed to Video Failure diagnostic chart

New build, CPU or RAM upgrade?
- No →
- Yes → Undo upgrade, confirm exact CPU, RAM model compatible with motherboard.

RAM reseated?
- Yes →
- No → Reseat RAM, minimize number of DIMMs, positive lever lock.

CPU seated flat?
- No → Reseat CPU and heatsink.
- Yes →

Freezes on boot?
- Yes →
- No → Proceed to Motherboard Performance chart.

Freezes bare bones?
- Yes →
- No → Restore one adapter or component at a time, unplugging or shutting off power strip each time, until culprit is detected.

Can you access BIOS?
- Yes →
- No →

CMOS settings default?
- Yes →
- No → Load defaults from BIOS, safe settings.

BIOS settings change?
- No →
- Yes → Remove motherboard battery, wait one hour.

Fan on heatsink active?
- Yes →
- No → Check fan power point, may not come on instantly at boot.

Temp and voltage stable?
- Yes →
- No → Replace heatsink if not certified, check power supply ripple.

More than one beep?
- No →
- Yes → Swap RAM, swap video.

RAM certified, tested?
- No → Check motherboard manufacturer website, swap or shuffle RAM.
- Yes →

Default motherboard settings?
- No → Restore factory motherboard settings.
- Yes →

Boots from CD or DVD?
- Yes → Proceed to Hard Drive Performance chart
- No → Proceed to Drive Failure chart

Runs on bench?
- Yes → Locate short, binding, or swap case.
- No →

CPU swap work?
- Yes → Bad CPU, watch voltage and heatsink on replacement.
- No → Motherboard or power supply bad.

Motherboard, RAM, CPU Failure

Does the PC start the boot process and get at least as far as displaying a message from the BIOS or any signs of life from Windows? If all you get is a text message telling you that the monitor can't detect a video signal, it doesn't count, since the monitor can display that message with no computer present.

Does the system power up? Do you hear any beeps, drives spinning up, fans, etc. If the power isn't coming on, proceed to Power Supply Failure flowchart. The power supply diagnostics will only send you back here if you are getting a definitive sign of life, in the form of a beep.

If you haven't performed the Video Failure diagnostics for a dead screen yet, do so now, and don't ignore the obvious steps, like checking the power cord and the outlet. You may be tempted to skip forward if you hear beeps, but there's no reason to assume at this point that beeps and the dead screen are the same problem.

Is this system a new build, or have you just upgraded any components? If you've just upgraded the hardware, power down, unplug the cord and swap the old components back one at a time. Check the motherboard manufacturer website to make sure that the exact CPU and memory modules (brand and specifications) are listed as compatible with the motherboard.

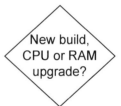

Of all the issues that can go wrong after you replace the motherboard or upgrade the memory, failure to install the memory modules properly is the most frequently encountered problem. Modern motherboards all use some form of DIMM (Dual Inline Memory Modules). All DIMM sockets are equipped with a locking lever on either end, and these levers must be opened (lowered) before inserting the DIMM, and should rise up and snap closed of their own accord as it seats. It can take quite a bit of force to seat a DIMM properly, but if you don't get it lined up first, you're going to damage the DIMM or the socket.

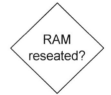

Depending on the motherboard design and the chipset used, motherboards can combine DIMMs to increase either performance or address space. Older designs used multiple banks to increase speed through interleaving or to "gang" 64 bit wide DIMMs together to create a 128 bit bus for the CPU. Newer "unganged" designs allow multi-core and multi-threading CPUs simultaneous and independent access to DIMMs. The DIMM sockets will be labeled or colored to show matching sockets for populating a bank or a channel, with up to four identical DIMMs required to populate an individual bank in quad channel designs. Further complicating issues is that some motherboard designs can treat multi-sided or multi-ranked DIMMs as if they were multiple DIMMs in the same bank, so see your motherboard documentation. In all cases, the DIMMs should be exactly matched, the same part from the same manufacturer. If different speeds are mixed, some mother-boards will fail to boot, the others will default all memory access to the lowest speed DIMM detected.

Even though DIMM memory is designed to exacting standards, the timing signals are so fussy that memory which has not been tested and approved for a particular motherboard will often fail. The speeds increase and the voltages fall with each new generation (initial releases of DDR4 were specified to operate at 1.20 V dropping to 1.05 V), so don't try to change the BIOS settings based on what you remember from an older PC. Generations of DDR memory are not backwards compatible and motherboards will only support one type. The DDR4 DIMM is up to 284 pins, compared to 240 pins for DDR3 and DDR2, and 184 pins for the original DDR DIMM. If your PC is more than twelve years old, you may have the obsolete RIMM (Rambus Inline Memory Module) memory which required CRIMMs (Continuity RIMMs) in empty slots. I don't remember the last time I saw a SIMM (Single Inline Memory Modules), but they were 16 bit, so 32 bit processors required matched pairs.

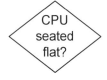

Illustrated CPU replacement:

www.fonerbooks.com /r_cpu.htm

The CPU version of faulty DIMM insertion is both harder to spot and harder to check. While memory modules can be popped in and out in a second, the massive heatsinks on today's high power processors are secured to the motherboard with strong spring clips that aren't designed for frequent operation. As the number of electrical contacts on CPU packages has soared above a thousand, Intel has largely dropped putting the pins on the CPU in favor of putting the pins in the socket, the LGA (Land Grid Array) design. AMD still uses PGA (Pin Grid Array) on some CPU packages, LGA on others.

LGA CPU's are more likely to sit flat and clamp down evenly than the older packages with pins or legs that could easily bind in the socket and hold one side of the CPU package out of contact while seemingly seated. Inspect the edges of the socket with a bright light and a small mirror if possible. If the heatsink obstructs your view completely, you can either remove the heatsink now to check and reseat the CPU, or you can continue troubleshooting, always remembering that you haven't done this test and that you certainly should before spending any money on replacement parts. With the CPU out, always inspect the bottom for discolorations and signs of melting or overheating, and check the socket (LGA) or the CPU (PGA) for bent or crushed pins.

Does the screen light up and the PC power on, only to freeze when the operating system begins to load? Some of the reasons a PC will freeze at the beginning of the boot process are different from those that cause freezes during normal operations, which we deal with on the motherboard performance flowchart. If you complete this flowchart and don't solve your boot problem, try the motherboard performance flowchart.

Does the system freeze when you strip it down to the minimum configuration required to start the boot process? This consists of the power supply, motherboard, CPU, the minimum required RAM, and a GPU (this can be an add-in video adapter, a video adapter integrated on the motherboard, or one of the newer CPU/GPU on a single chip solutions). You can also leave the primary hard drive connected for the first try, though powering up without a hard drive should result in a missing boot device error message rather than a frozen BIOS screen on a healthy PC.

If your system failed with a popping noise or a smoky smell before the freeze-up happened, do your best to locate the failed component by visual inspection (and smell) before you reassemble the PC. If the system boots, or at least passes the point of the freeze-up when it's stripped down, you can start replacing the parts one-by-one, always remembering to unplug the power supply or turn off the power strip when replacing motherboard adapters. When the freeze up returns after you replace a part, you've found the culprit, but double check that the issue is with the component and not with the motherboard slot or the power connector by trying the part in another slot or on another power lead.

Are you able to access the BIOS (CMOS Setup) by pressing the hot key(s)? The most common hot keys are F2 or Del, but there are dozens of possibilities with older PCs, including multiple keys held down simultaneously, including the CTRL and ALT keys. Most BIOS will normally flash the CMOS Setup hotkey(s) as a text message on the screen at the beginning of the boot

process, but some major manufacturers suppressed this to discourage owners from altering the settings and creating a tech support headache. You can always find the key combination through a patient Internet search with the brand and model of your PC. If you cannot access the BIOS settings, the diagnostic approach is the same as it would be with a dead screen, and you should review the dead screen steps before proceeding.

Did you change the BIOS settings (CMOS Setup) or flash the BIOS (replace it with a newer BIOS version) immediately before the failure occurred? If you were playing with your timing settings for the memory to try to boost performance or clear up a random freeze, or if you were overclocking, odds are your most recent setting is preventing boot. If you can't access the BIOS, the only solution is to clear the settings so that the BIOS will insert the default values for safe operation on the next power up. See your motherboard manual because there are many different approaches to clearing the settings and the wrong approach could damage your motherboard.

Some motherboards provide a jumper or motherboard button for clearing the nonvolatile memory in a few seconds, though you must unplug the power supply first. Otherwise, you need to locate and remove the motherboard battery, unplug the power supply, and let it stand for a good hour or two to let the battery backed settings dissipate. Some manufacturers will suggest you short across the motherboard terminals for the battery after it's removed. The procedures vary according to whether BIOS settings are stored in battery backed CMOS (the old scheme from which CMOS Setup got its name), in an EEPROM, or integrated in the chipset. If you get desperate, see YouTube for CMOS clearing hacks.

A stone dead CPU is another reason for a system to fail. All modern CPUs require a heatsink, and these are active heatsinks, with a fan on top. You may encounter a heatsink without a fan in an old mass-manufactured brand-name PC, but those were much less powerful CPUs. Check the action on all motherboard mounted heatsink fans There may be a heatsink fan on the chipset (the Northbridge handles communications between the memory and graphics systems and the CPU so it can run very hot) or a motherboard integrated GPU.

The heatsink fan must be hooked up to the correct power point on the motherboard for the BIOS to monitor its condition and turn it off and on. Depending on the BIOS programming, the CPU fan may not spin up immediately when the system is powered on because the CPU is cold. While CPUs should be able to shut themselves down to prevent thermal self destruction, if you just installed a new CPU and powered the system up with no heatsink at all, it may be too late for the CPU.

If the fan on your active heatsink doesn't spin up, replace it (clean the heatsink and CPU and reapply thermal compound) and hope for the best. Avoid prying when removing the heatsink, twist it back and forth after the retention mechanism is removed to break the adhesion of the thermal compound. If you don't trust the power point on the motherboard, it won't hurt the CPU to run a fan directly from a power supply lead through a "Y" adapter, so it comes on instantly and always stays on. Just make sure that the fan can tolerate the voltage, and realize that if you replace a PWM (Pulse Width Modulation) controlled fan with a full-on constant DC voltage fan, the background noise from the PC will be louder.

Make sure that the geometry of the bottom of the heatsink will bring it in full contact with the exposed CPU die or the top of the CPU package. Apply an approved thermal grease or thermal tape before reinstalling the heatsink. Don't put on too much thermal grease or you'll just make a mess. The thermal media is only there to fill the microscopic gaps between the die surface and the heatsink. Don't improvise your thermal material, go to a computer or electronics store and buy some if it didn't come with the parts you purchased online. Installing heatsinks can be frustrating, but this isn't a "bash away at it" process. You can damage the CPU if you start cracking the heatsink against it in an attempt to get the heatsink to sit right. Be patient, study the mechanical connections, make sure you aren't hitting some poorly placed component on the motherboard and check that your heatsink isn't so oversized it just won't fit on the particular motherboard. Just because a heatsink is certified to work with a CPU doesn't mean it's certified to fit on a particular motherboard design.

Do you hear more than one beep from the system on power up? You should hear a single short beep, not a long, continual beep that can mean that the required auxiliary power isn't connected to a video adapter. Note that very old PCs used the case speaker, rather than an onboard piezoelectric for beep codes, so you won't hear anything unless the case speaker is attached to the

More than one beep?

four pin speaker block (the outside two pins were used) on the motherboard.

If you hear an unending string of beeps, it's often bad RAM (or a stuck key on the keyboard after boot), while a repeated sequence can be RAM or video. Other beep codes have been largely abandoned since they pertained to what are non-user replaceable surface mount components today. Beeps or no beeps, I always reseat the video adapter and the RAM, paying special attention to the locking levers on the memory sockets.

If you have more than one DIMM installed on a motherboard that only requires one DIMM to boot, try swapping your RAM through the first slot, one DIMM at a time. Read up on your motherboard's use of ganged and unganged, single or double-sided DIMMs (which no longer literally means chips on both sides) and alternating banks to determine the permissible arrangements. It's also a good time to try known good working RAM from another PC that uses the same technology if you have access to some. If the RAM currently installed doesn't meet the motherboard manufacturer specs or isn't on their approved list, it's suspect, even if it worked in the past. Improperly selected RAM can be the cause of problems ranging from no-boot to intermittent lock-ups.

You can try to clean the DIMM slots with a soft cloth or a can of compressed air, just make sure you aren't leaving threads, hairs or dust in the slot when you are done, because it doesn't take a lot of insulation to break a contact. While you'll rarely see this today, if a PC uses tinned (silver color) contacts against gold contacts, the dissimilar metals can cause corrosion over time due to a constant electrical current when the power is off.

Check your motherboard documentation to determine whether there are any jumpers or switch blocks used for operational settings. With the exception of a jumper for clearing CMOS Setup, these are obsolete today (replaced with CMOS Setup settings), but they were still in wide use with early ATX PCs, some of which are still in use today.

Running the motherboard without a case is a common technique used by technicians to eliminate any weird grounding or unintended shorting issues or mechanical stresses. It also makes it much easier to swap the CPU if that's required. I normally do my bench testing on top of a cardboard box, with a static free bag or foam between the bottom of the motherboard and the cardboard. You don't walk away from a test like this or you might come back to find the box on fire! If your motherboard powers up on the bench with the same power supply that you used in the case, you have a geometry problem. Ideally, you should have a spare power supply for bench testing if you're going to do regular repair and testing work.

Make sure some standoffs aren't higher than others, putting unacceptable stress on the motherboard. Check that every standoff appears under a screw hole. The easiest way to be sure is to count the standoffs, count the screws, and make sure there are no screws leftover after you install the motherboard. There could be a short caused by a misplaced standoff, a loose screw, metal chips from shoddy materials. I've encountered standoff shorts that produce an endless string of beeps like RAM failure, without damaging the motherboard. There's also the possibility that the case geometry is so messed up (out of square or out of level when the cover is forced on) that it's putting an unacceptable mechanical stress on the motherboard, resulting in an open circuit. If you can't find the cause of the problem, don't hesitate to try another case and power supply.

Illustrated motherboard installation:

www.fonerbooks.com /r_board.htm

If you still have a "no power" situation with the motherboard running out of the case, there's always the last refuge of a scoundrel. Swap in a known good CPU, not forgetting to install a good heatsink and to connect the fan, even just for a quick test. I try to keep around some cheaper CPUs for this purpose, just in case the motherboard is a CPU eater. You can usually find very inexpensive CPUs for sale on eBay as "pulls," removed from PCs with other problems, and you should try the lowest speed CPU (lowest cost) of the family that your motherboard supports. It's another good reason to leave all the motherboard settings on the default "Automatic" setting, so you don't have to fool around with them at this stage.

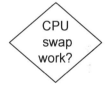

CPU swap work?

If your old CPU is bad and the heatsink fan is dead, it's a pretty good bet that the dead fan caused the CPU failure. If the heatsink fan is working, determining whether the CPU failure was due to poor heatsink contact, improper motherboard settings (overclocking), or lousy power regulation from the motherboard is a guessing game. If the motherboard is an older make and you have a couple bucks to spare, replace the CPU and the motherboard together. Replacing just the CPU, even if the motherboard tests out OK, is kind of risky and usually tough to justify from a price/performance standpoint unless the system was practically new, say less than a year old.

Illustrated motherboard removal:

www.fonerbooks.com /r_mother.htm

If you still have no beeps and no video, you're probably looking at a bad motherboard. But unless you have a DVM and the experience to check the live power supply voltages at the motherboard through back-picking the connectors, I would first try swapping the power supply (if you have access to one) just because it's easier. Again, this diagnosis assumes that you went through the Video Failure diagnostics, which would have forced you through the Power Supply Failure diagnostics as well. Get the PC operating with a replacement motherboard and all the identical parts that the old motherboard failed with before you make the trash can decision.

If you aren't using the default CMOS settings, try restoring the factory settings. Even if you don't remember ever changing any advanced settings for the chipset, memory timing or CPU, it's a good idea to just restore the defaults at this point. You can usually restore these from a major CMOS Setup menu item like "Restore Default Settings" or "BIOS Default Settings." The default settings usually put everything on autodetect and use the recommended timing for the RAM. This means if you're overclocking, stop it, at least until you get the system running again. It doesn't matter whether or not overclocking the exact same CPU or RAM in a friend's system worked without a hitch, you're exceeding the manufacturers recommendations so it's a gamble.

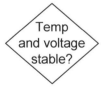

Are the temperature and supply voltages stable? The BIOS monitors CPU temperature and reports various supply voltages, in some cases using these measurements to determine whether to shut down the PC for thermal overload or voltage instability. These settings can usually be viewed through CMOS Setup, and for future reference, you can access them with 3rd party tools from Windows as well. If your CPU supports DTS (an Internet search will tell you), make sure that the temperature you see displayed is based on DTS and not on a thermocouple that may or may not have good thermal contact with the CPU.

The low voltages (less than 3.3 V) are created on by the motherboard using higher voltages from the power supply, so if the power supply output is stable and the memory voltage is wandering around, the fault lies on the motherboard. If the temperature proves to be unstable, see the text associated with the "Fan on heatsink active?" decision point which addresses the issues involved with reinstalling the heatsink.

Is the brand and model number of the RAM installed in the PC certified and tested to work with the motherboard? The days are gone when you could assume that if the notches in the DIMM matched the keys in the DIMM sockets, the memory would work. The high performance demanded from today's memory requires increasingly exquisite timing that isn't always achieved by adherence to a general specification. Check the motherboard manufacturer website to see if the RAM you are using is explicitly listed as being tested with the motherboard and CPU.

If you have more RAM installed than is required to boot, it's a good idea to shuffle the DIMMs in and out of the PC to see if there was a problem DIMM causing the freeze up once the operating system started loading. And if you have access to RAM that is compatible with your motherboard, even if it's slower than the DIMMs you are using, try swapping it in for the sake of process of elimination.

Does the system boot from a CD or DVD, or from a bootable memory stick? In order to run this test, you may have to enter CMOS Setup and change the boot order to set the CD, DVD or USB memory stick as the first boot device. Otherwise, the BIOS will continue trying to boot from a corrupted hard drive (if that's the problem) and the system will freeze rather than going on to try booting from other devices.

If the PC boots from an alternative device, the problem is most likely data corruption, either with the hard drive's master boot (MBR) record or with the operating system. You can test whether the hard drive data is still accessible by exiting to the command prompt from a bootable Windows disc, rather than trying to repair the installation or do a fresh Windows install. If you can access some or all of the data, you can add the drive to a bootable PC as a second hard drive and then either burn the data to DVD or copy it to the host hard drive. See the Hard Drive Performance flowchart for possible causes and solutions.

If the system won't boot from a CD or DVD, proceed to the ATA Drive Failure flowchart. Note that older system with the CMOS option to boot from a USB memory device were often finicky about it, so it's safer to use an original operating system disc for the test.

Motherboard, CPU, RAM Performance

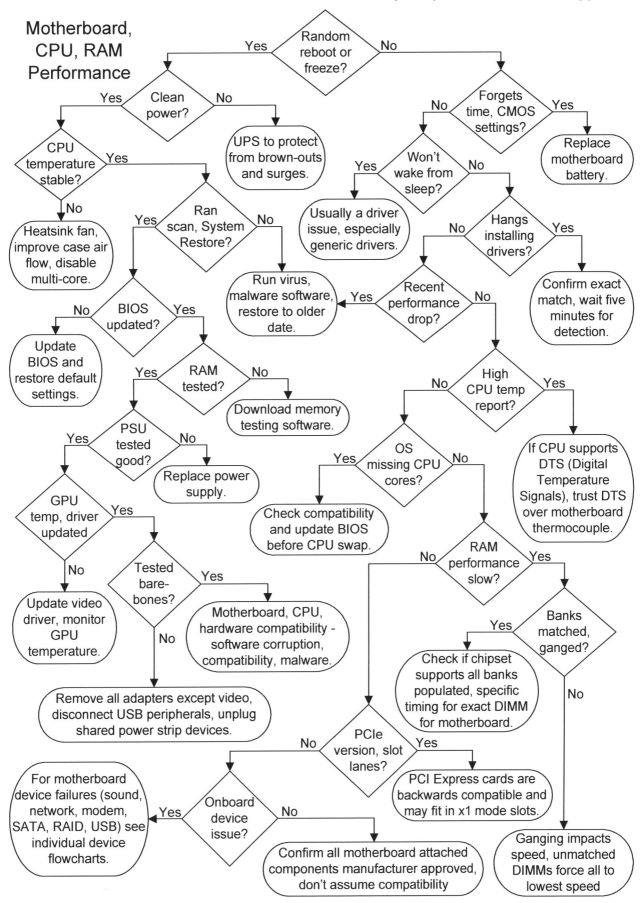

Random reboot or freeze?

Yes → **Clean power?**
- Yes → **CPU temperature stable?**
  - Yes → **Ran scan, System Restore?**
  - No → Heatsink fan, improve case air flow, disable multi-core.
- No → UPS to protect from brown-outs and surges.

No → **Forgets time, CMOS settings?**
- Yes → Replace motherboard battery.
- No → **Won't wake from sleep?**
  - Yes → Usually a driver issue, especially generic drivers.
  - No → **Hangs installing drivers?**
    - Yes → Confirm exact match, wait five minutes for detection.
    - No → **Recent performance drop?**

Ran scan, System Restore?
- Yes → **BIOS updated?**
  - No → Update BIOS and restore default settings.
  - Yes → **RAM tested?**
    - Yes → **PSU tested good?**
      - Yes → **GPU temp, driver updated**
        - Yes → **Tested bare-bones?**
          - Yes → Motherboard, CPU, hardware compatibility - software corruption, compatibility, malware.
          - No → Remove all adapters except video, disconnect USB peripherals, unplug shared power strip devices.
        - No → Update video driver, monitor GPU temperature.
      - No → Replace power supply.
    - No → Download memory testing software.
- No → Run virus, malware software, restore to older date.

Recent performance drop?
- Yes → Run virus, malware software, restore to older date.
- No → **High CPU temp report?**
  - Yes → If CPU supports DTS (Digital Temperature Signals), trust DTS over motherboard thermocouple.
  - No → **OS missing CPU cores?**
    - Yes → Check compatibility and update BIOS before CPU swap.
    - No → **RAM performance slow?**
      - Yes → **Banks matched, ganged?**
        - Yes → Check if chipset supports all banks populated, specific timing for exact DIMM for motherboard.
        - No → Ganging impacts speed, unmatched DIMMs force all to lowest speed
      - No → **PCIe version, slot lanes?**
        - Yes → PCI Express cards are backwards compatible and may fit in x1 mode slots.
        - No → **Onboard device issue?**
          - Yes → For motherboard device failures (sound, network, modem, SATA, RAID, USB) see individual device flowcharts.
          - No → Confirm all motherboard attached components manufacturer approved, don't assume compatibility

Motherboard, CPU, RAM Performance

Does the system reboot itself for no apparent reason, either during the boot process or at any point once you're up and running? Random reboots and freezes are often caused by mechanical or thermal problems. However, keep in mind that an inadvertent power management setting may be sending your system into sleep mode after one minute of inactivity. A corrupted operating system or a virus can also cause repeated reboots or freeze-ups, as can the power supply and bad memory. We'll work through these by process of elimination.

I've seen bad power supplies that cause a system to reboot if somebody walks across the room or sets a coffee cup down on the table. But people are often quick to blame the power supply for random issues that are actually caused by problems with the electric utility distribution system that the power supply is drawing on. If you live somewhere with frequent brown-outs (the brightness of incandescent light bulbs will droop noticeably), or with frequent fluctuations in the distribution voltage caused by demand from large industrial facilities, or with off-the-grid power from a variety of alternative energy solutions, the fix may be to purchase a quality UPS (uninterruptible power supply) that protects from surges and brown-outs. It also makes sense to use a simple plug-in tester to see if the circuits in your house are properly grounded.

Is the CPU temperature stable? If the CPU temperature continues to rise and nears the maximum allowed by the manufacturer, it will usually result in a reboot or lock-up as the CPU shuts down to protect itself. If the fan on the CPU heatsink never spins up, you've found the problem and can probably replace the fan without replacing the heatsink. Also remember that a working fan's ability to cool the heatsink depends on the temperature of the air in the case, so if the case fans have failed or are blocked, or if intake and exhaust fans are working against each other (both doing intake or exhaust) the air temperature is probably too high for efficient CPU cooling. The same is true for running in hot weather without air conditioning. If you need to replace the fan and heatsink, see the text for "Fan and heatsink active?" in the Motherboard, CPU and RAM failure chapter.

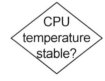

If you have a multi-core CPU, another option is to disable one or more of the cores to see if that cures the overheating problem.

While you may be unwilling to live with a CPU that performs below its potential, it's a great troubleshooting step because it can pin the problem squarely on CPU overheating. If the CPU and GPU are combined on the same chip, you can also try disabling the GPU and using an add-in graphics adapter as a test.

Have you run a full virus and malware scan with an updated security suite and have you tried setting the system back to a pre-problem Windows restore point? An author could write a much fatter book than this one simply about software issues that can cause random glitches, but our focus in this book is hardware, so we can only treat software issues with a big hammer.

First, update your security suite or prepare a bootable DVD or memory stick with the latest trial software from a reputable anti-virus company and do a full scan. This can take several hours if you have a lot of stuff on your hard drive. If the security scan doesn't turn up any problems, it doesn't necessarily mean that you're in the clear, just that it's nothing obvious.

Next, on Windows systems starting with XP, you can run System Restore from the System Tools, which is buried in the Programs menu under Accessories. System Restore is not a panacea, it often runs through the restoration process only to announce on reboot that the restoration attempt has failed, but I've never had it leave a system in worse shape than it started. Sometimes choosing a different Restore point will fix the problem, but other times you'll find that System Restore simply won't run to completion due to some conflicting software that's been installed. Microsoft online support is actually helpful in these cases if the operating system is still supported.

If you don't have automatic Windows updates turned on, visit the Microsoft website and install their tool that will check the status of your operating system and download and install all of the patches required. This can be a lengthy process, especially if you've just reinstalled an older operating system that requires several service pack updates before it can even get to the latest patches. If Microsoft abandons support for a particular configuration, as they did with the original Windows XP years before abandoning support for the last XP version, you may need to find the service pack to update your factory installation disc before you can make use of Microsoft's update tool.

Another test is to boot in Safe Mode and see if the problems go away. If so, you can be pretty confident that the issue is software. Try updating any drivers, and if the problem started after you installed a new program or a new piece of hardware, by all means remove it and see if the problem clears up. You can also try reinstalling Windows which usually won't affect your data (pictures, documents, etc), though you may have trouble with some installed programs, but Windows is pretty good about warning you if a repair or reinstallation effort is likely make things worse.

If you haven't updated the BIOS in a long time (or ever), do an Internet search to see if the motherboard manufacturer or chipset maker has a new version that has been tested with your motherboard. Remember that your operating system has likely been updated several times since the original BIOS was created, not to mention new hardware coming on the market that didn't exist when your motherboard was manufactured, even though the standards indicated the new hardware would be supported. Flashing the BIOS may clear up any problems you are having, but take heed of any warnings about the flash process and ensuring that the BIOS upgrade is compatible with your motherboard lest a blown update leaves you with a brick.

Have you run a software based memory test? Download a free memory testing tool from a reputable website and allow it to run as long as required to thoroughly test the installed RAM. Unlike a hard drive, which can tolerate and hide a certain number of hardware errors through dynamic reallocation, memory modules must test out as error free.

Have you done everything within your means to test the power supply? Start with the crude tests you can do easily, like tapping on the power supply to see if it causes the system to reboot, and moving the computer to a different circuit in the house. If you've noticed the PC locking-up or rebooting when your old laser printer cycles on or when it gets cold and your electric heater comes into use, it could be that the circuit the power supply is plugged into is experiencing its own private brown-outs.

Very few people own a power supply tester and repair shops usually do without them because most only test whether the correct voltage appears on each output, without varying the load or detecting ripple. If you are comfortable with using a DVM on live circuitry in an open case, you can measure the voltages through the top of the ATX connector if there's room. An accurate picture of AC ripple on a DC voltage really requires an oscilloscope, but some sophisticated multimeters may do a decent job if used properly. See the last text section of the power supply troubleshooting chapter for testing suggestions.

Have you upgraded the graphics adapter drivers to the latest version and confirmed that it's cooling properly? The latest software drivers may be necessary to work with software that has been released since the original drivers were installed. For OEM (generic) video cards, you can usually obtain driver updates through the GPU makers website (Nvidia, AMD Radeon), Intel (chipset and integrated CPU/GPU). A video BIOS update is rarely necessary, and I wouldn't do one without an explicit suggestion from the manufacturer. Most of the video BIOS update information you'll find on the Internet is generated by and for overclockers.

High performance GPUs monitor their own temperatures and report the temperature out to the configuration and control software provided by the manufacturer. GPU temperature will vary greatly in accordance with the tasks being performed, with gaming and certain engineering modeling applications causing the greatest sustained temperature spikes. Of course, if the fan on the GPU heatsink has failed, you can expect the temperature to run away and eventually cause the GPU to throttle back performance to protect itself, and failing that, overheat and sustain damage.

If you have a dual graphics card system, one of the cards will be further from the power supply and auxiliary case fan than the other, and will see appreciably less air flow. Motherboard manufacturers generally have the sense to space their SLI or CrossFire compatible PCI Express slots as far apart as real estate allows, but if the cooling fan on the second card ends up a fraction of an inch from the back of the first card, you know it's begging for overheating problems. Some graphics adapters use two slot spaces at the back of the case, with one serving as the exhaust port for a doublewide fan/heatsink system.

Have you tested the system in minimal bare-bones configuration, both hardware and software? Normally when we talk about bare-bones, we mean the minimal hardware configuration required to test against a particular problem. Bare-bones testing for a no-video condition when you power on doesn't require a hard drive while bare-bones testing for no-boot does. The hardware bare-bones test is easy to do, so strip the PC down to the minimum required to boot and get Windows loaded, and see if your random freezes or reboots go away. If so, you can rebuild a component at a time to find the culprit.

But if the problem isn't due to hardware such as RAM, the power supply or an add-in video adapter, possibilities you were able to eliminate through bare-bones testing or swapping with known good components, you're left looking at the motherboard and CPU and guessing that one could be defective. If the CPU isn't overheating, it's more likely the motherboard, but another major possibility is software.

There are two basic options for testing bare-bones software. The first is to boot in Safe Mode and try to keep yourself busy playing in Windows Paint or some other innocuous software for long enough to see if your random reboot or freeze is going to repeat. If the PC now tests OK, it either means that you have software corruption, conflicts, a malware infestation, or that the particular game you were playing or Internet site you were visiting whenever the PC froze was responsible.

The second and more thorough way to test bare-bones software is to swap in a new hard drive and do a fresh operating system installation. Don't connect to the Internet, pick a single task like playing a movie DVD to keep the PC busy, and see if the problem clears up. If it does, connect to the Internet and let all of the Windows updates install, and give it a day to see if the PC remains stable. Then you can start reinstalling all of your necessary applications, and try to restrain yourself from loading the PC up immediately with software you don't use every day. Either you will eventually get everything installed and the PC will run great, which means the problem was software corruption or malware, or the problem will return, which will tell you that the most recent software installed is the problem.

Does the system clock keep losing the date and time, or does the system ever enter CMOS Setup for no apparent reason? Some ancient desktop boards may even give a "Low Battery" warning at boot. Some motherboards have a replaceable battery likely to be a large watch type battery, though universal replacements for any given voltage are available. The battery really shouldn't fail during the usable life of the PC, so if it does, the problem may turn out to be that something is causing it to drain too quickly. If

Forgets time, CMOS settings?

the forgotten CMOS settings are stored in an EEPROM, then the EEPROM replacing, a new battery won't help.

Does the PC go to sleep from your choice on the Shut Down menu, from the "sleep" key on an enhanced keyboard, or from power saver settings, and then fail to wake up when you move the mouse, hit a key, or press the power switch, depending on whether it's sleep or stand-by? You may see a similar issue with a screensaver not giving up the desktop despite keyboard activity. The issue is usually conflicting software drivers or the need to patch a driver. Start with keyboard, mouse and motherboard drivers, and if you upgraded any hardware or installed a new program recently, try undoing the change for the sake of testing.

Does the PC hang up when you are installing a new driver? This isn't the same as a true freeze, as you can usually access the task list (Ctrl-Alt-Del) and close the driver installation window. But the problem remains if it's a required driver and you are unable to install it, especially if it's the initial motherboard or graphics adapter drivers as opposed to an update. The first step is to just wait, it may take five minutes or more for the software to complete its hardware detection and assessment process.

Next, make sure that the driver you have downloaded or received on DVD actually matches the hardware you have installed. Manufacturer websites often do a poor job of guiding you to the correct driver or update for your installed hardware, especially if the components are generic and you are relying on a driver from the chipset maker rather than the component manufacturer. If the driver fails to install from the manufacturer DVD, check the DVD for scratches and if possible, see if you can obtain the same software from the manufacturer website. If you only have it on DVD, also see the DVD performance flowchart for possible issues.

If the driver software is downloaded from the Internet, try downloading it again. Corrupted downloads are more common than people think, the error checking depends on the download type and it's not perfect in any case. It's also possible that the manufacturer has recently posted a driver that hasn't been extensively tested for compatibility, so see if they allow you to download a previous version.

Did PC performance degrade noticeably in a short span of time in recent days or weeks? The answer here is usually malware, though it can also be something as simple as the hard drive filling up and the operating system running out of room for swapping memory to disk. Right click on your C: drive symbol in Windows (My Computer and other locations) and click properties to ensure that free space is at least 10% of the drive. I recommend against allowing compression to save space. Take the time to delete files you are no longer using or archive them on DVD. Rather than repeating an entire page of text here, see the suggested actions for answering "No" to "Ran scan, System Restore?" a couple pages back.

Are you seeing high CPU temperatures reported in CMOS Setup or through a monitoring utility after boot, without suffering from lock-ups or reboots? CPU's didn't always offer DTS (Digital Thermal Sensors or Digital Temperature Signaling depending on the manufacturer), and motherboards included a thermocouple to read the CPU temperature by contact. Before you get worried about a high CPU temperature, make sure that it is generated by DTS and not a thermocouple that can't actually measure the temperature inside the processor die.

Both multi-core CPUs and CPUs that integrate the GPU on the same chip may only record a single temperature. In this case, you may see widely varying readings depending on the loading of the cores and the GPU, and you may be able to prevent overheating by switching to an add-in graphics adapter or disabling one or more CPU cores through the operating system.

Does your operating system fail to individually register all of the cores of your multi-core CPU? Rather than assuming hardware failure, which is very rare, start by making sure that multi-core operation hasn't been disabled. A quick Internet search will get you instructions for enabling or disabling cores for your particular operating system. If the cores are enabled, you may need to update both the BIOS and the motherboard drivers. If you've upgraded a single core processor with a multi-core, you may have to jump through some hoops to get them all working. Search the Microsoft Forums, and be warned ahead of time that some people just give up and reinstall Windows from scratch.

Are you seeing lower than expected speed for your installed RAM on the boot splash screen or through memory testing software? There are a number of reasons for RAM to underperform its specifications, from being installed in

combinations the motherboard doesn't recognize to improper settings in CMOS Setup. For example, some motherboards offer more DIMM sockets than the chipset supports at top speed, resulting in all memory operations defaulting to a lower speed if every socket is populated. See your motherboard manual for details.

Are the DIMMs exactly matched and are the DIMMs within each bank ganged? While motherboard specifications generally allow for different DIMMs using the same speed chips and the identical technology (single sided, double sided), it's much safer to use DIMMs that are exactly matched, by speed, brand, and circuit card generation. All of the DIMMs on the motherboard should ideally be identical, and certainly the DIMMs within a single bank. And in most cases, the motherboard will detect the lowest speed DIMM and force all memory operations to default to that speed.

Whether or not ganging DIMMs in banks will increase performance depends on the CPU's memory bus as not all CPUs can take advantage of 128 bit or even 192 bit (triple ganged DIMMs) wide memory. And it's important that the BIOS settings for memory and chipset timing are all correct, they may not be autodetected. Ganging was seen as a step up from the old interleaving (memory banks have been around forever), but modern multi-core CPUs probably benefit more from unganged operation where the DIMMs are divvied up between the cores.

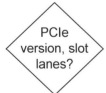

Do the PCI Express versions of the PCIe adapters you are using match the PCIe version of the motherboard slots, and are the adapters in slots that run the proper number of lanes? Five different revisions of PCI Express (1.0a, 1.1, 2.0, 2.1 and 3.0) have been used in PCs and you may still encounter adapters and motherboard slots that only support the early versions. PCIe 4.0 is scheduled but wasn't available at press time. Each major revision of the PCIe standard has doubled, or nearly doubled the transfer rate of each serial bus lane, and each slot offers from 1 to 16 lanes depending on the design.

Adapters have generally been backwards compatible in terms of fitting in slots of the rated lane width (x1, x4, x8, x16), but were not always backwards compatible with their power demands. Motherboards with PCI Express 1.1 slots may have a BIOS update available to handle the requirements of 2.1 and higher adapters, but performance will be limited to PCIe 1.0. The performance increase from PCI Express 2.0 or 2.1 to 3.0 won't generally be seen by users since bandwidth was not yet an issue for PCIe 2.0 adapters when PCIe 3.0 adapters became available.

The more lanes a PCIe slot requires, the more expensive it is to add that slot to a motherboard. In order to physically support multiple high performance adapters, motherboard makers can save money while offering a full complement of high capacity slots, but not provide the motherboard circuitry to run all of the lanes. So you might see a motherboard indentify slots as x4 (x1) or x16 (x8) which means they accept a x4 adapter and run it as x1, or allow you to install an x16 adapter, but only provide x8 support in the slot. Note also that some older motherboards designed for AMD CrossFire or nVidia SLI required a terminator, sometimes called a PCIe switch, to be installed in the empty x16 slot if only one x16 slot was used.

A less sophisticated approach taken by some motherboard makers is to leave the end of lower performance (x1, x4, x8) slots open, so that a higher performance adapter can be installed with the end hanging out in space. Some adapters will correctly sense the number of available lanes and adjust down, but performance will be limited by the number of lanes. And make sure that the exposed contacts on the free edge of the adapter aren't in danger of contacting any motherboard components.

Do you have a problem with any of the motherboard integrated I/O (sound, network, keyboard or mouse ports, modem, USB) or with PATA or SATA drive controllers? For all of the above, refer to the relevant flowchart (mouse, keyboard and USB are included under the general category of peripherals). Every one of these motherboard functions can be upgraded or replaced with inexpensive add-in adapters, providing you have open motherboard slots and can disable the motherboard device.

Onboard device issue?

If you've reached this point in the flowchart and you haven't found your complaint, try looking through the other performance flowcharts that may relate to the problem. Also, make sure that any of the hardware involved is approved by the motherboard manufacturer, and upgrade the motherboard BIOS if the manufacturer is still in business and an update is available. For older no-name motherboards, you may just be out of luck, and all manufacturers eventually abandon support for PC components, so you may be unable to get a perfectly good component to function properly under the latest Windows. Microsoft also abandons support for their older Windows versions as the years pass, so you can't run a PC forever unless you keep it off the Internet and don't try to upgrade components.

It's always possible that the components you have installed are too new for the BIOS to know what to make of them or for the motherboard to take advantage of their capabilities. Sometimes the BIOS will identify the component correctly, like a CPU or a hard drive, but will only operate it at the highest speed or capacity that the motherboard is capable of. This problem isn't anybody's fault, it's just not possible for motherboard manufacturers to be prepared for everything that may come down the pike in the next couple years. Not to mention testing compliance with hardware that doesn't exist yet.

ATA Drive
Failure

ATA Drive Failure

Are all installed ATA drives properly identified by the BIOS and displayed on the start-up screen? Any modern PC should be able to identify the drive by model number, brand, capacity, and usually the transfer mode. Some brand name PCs may not display a start-up BIOS registration screen, so you'll have to enter CMOS Setup to view the information. If the key stroke required to enter CMOS Setup isn't displayed on the screen as the PC begins to boot, you'll need to look it up in the documentation or on the Internet. Common keys used to access CMOS Setup at boot are, <DEL>, <F1> and <F2>.

Is it a solid state drive (SSD)? While SSDs with ATA interfaces should look like their mechanical counterparts to the BIOS, they have some distinctive characteristics from the troubleshooting standpoint. Namely, they don't have motors, read/write heads on a moving arm, or spinning discs. So they don't make any noise and they don't resist twisting like a gyroscope. In case of a failed SSD firmware update, power down your PC completely, remove the cord, and let it sit for an hour, then try powering up and down a few more times to see if the drive will appear in the BIOS.

Is the SSD drive equipped with a SATA or PATA (IDE) interface? In terms of cabling issues for power and data, and jumpers for addressing, troubleshooting SSD drives when they are interfaced as PATA or SATA drives is the same as for the magnetic drives. But one of the main failure modes for an SSD drive is simply not showing up in the BIOS. The very next time you power down and power up again, the drive might reappear, but I would take that as an opportunity to back up any important data and return the drive if it's under warranty.

Some SSD drives are sold with a PCIe (PCI Express) interface, but configuring these as the boot drive can be tricky or impossible. If you're just looking for faster boot time, a SATA 3 SSD may make more sense. SSD drives also come with USB and SCSI interfaces, plus a couple more exotic interfaces only used in servers. For the main part, you troubleshoot SSD devices the same way you would any device with the same interface. So for USB SSD, see the general USB troubleshooting guidelines in the Peripherals flowchart and for SCSI SSD see the SCSI flowchart. For PCIe SSD, after reseating the PCIe card, check for known conflicts with the video adapter. Make sure the motherboard PCIe version supports the SSD card, and that the PCIe slot has the full number of lanes (x8, x16). Update the drivers from the manufacturer and check if they require a firmware update.

Does the hard drive spin up? We covered this in the power supply diagnostics, but I'll repeat it here for convenience. When the PC powers up, you should hear the hard drive motor spinning up the drive and the gentle clunking sound of the read/write head seeking. If I can't tell whether or not the drive is spinning up, even with my fingers on the drive's top cover, I run the drive in my hand. A spun up drive resists a slow twisting movement just like a gyroscope. Don't flip it quickly or play with it or you may damage the drive, not to mention touching the circuitry against a conductor and causing a short. Just power down, put the drive back in and continue with the diagnostics.

Illustrated PATA hard drive replacement:

www.fonerbooks.com /r_hard.htm

One of the reasons you should always use four screws in older PATA drives is so you can push hard on the power connector without the unit shifting around and possibly damaging the circuit board. I've never broken a power socket off the circuit board on a hard drive, but I've seen it done, so don't go too crazy on it. Try the hard drive in another PC or a USB shell before you conclude that it's dead.

The diagnostic tree splits here between the newer SATA (Serial ATA) interface drives and the older PATA (Parallel ATA) interface drives. PATA drives are often referred to as plain "ATA" or "IDE," the terms refer to the same technology. SATA and PATA drives feature different connectors for both for power and data, so you can't hook the wrong drive up to the wrong interface. On the SATA drives, the power cable is wider than the data cable, on the older PATA or IDE drives, the data cable is a wide ribbon cable and the power cable is an old fashioned Molex 4 wire connector (also used by some early SATA 1 drives).

The initial interface speed for SATA drives was 150 MB/s, also known as SATA 1. The next generation SATA 2 interface supports 300 MB/s and the current SATA 3 peaks around 600 MB/s. Since the "S" in SATA stands for serial, the specification actually describes a bit rate, 1.5 Gbits/s for SATA 1, 3.0 Gbits/s for SATA 2, and 6.0 Gbits/s for SATA 3, but hard drive transfer rates are traditionally described with the more useful MB/s that I use here. If you are replacing an older SATA drive with one from a newer generation and it isn't recognized by the BIOS or won't boot reliably, check if the drive has an onboard compatibility jumper that will slow down the interface for it to work properly with a SATA 1 controller designed for a 150 MB/s peak transfer rate, or a SATA 2 controller designed for a 300 MB/s peak transfer rate.

The SATA interface is pretty bullet-proof in comparison with the older IDE technology, you almost have to work at getting the cabling or jumpers wrong. If the drive powers up but isn't recognized by the BIOS, it's possible that the data cable is bad, or not properly seated on either the drive or the motherboard. If the data cable is known to be good (you saw it work in another system), try attaching it to a different SATA port on the motherboard. Some motherboards offer a completely separate set of SATA connectors for RAID arrays (see hard drive performance). If the motherboard BIOS supports AHCI (Advanced Host Controller Interface) you should enable it, otherwise the SATA drive will end up emulating an IDE drive if it works. If Windows is already installed, see the "Just switched to AHCI?" decision point on the Hard Drive Performance and Boot chart.

Any time two old IDE drives share a single cable, the computer needs a way to tell them apart. This can be accomplished by using jumpers on the drives to set one to "Master" and the other to "Slave" or through selection by the cable. The Master/Slave setting is set by jumpers, usually on the back end of the drive between the power socket and the IDE connector. The labeling for the jumpers is usually in shorthand, "M" for Master and "S" for Slave. Some older drives include a jumper for "Single" (and spelled out labels) for when the drive is the only drive installed on the ribbon. Since pre-SATA motherboards always supported both a primary and a secondary IDE interface, it's not necessary with a two drive system to hang them both on the same cable. The boot hard drive should always be the Master on the primary IDE interface. If the CD, DVD, or any other IDE drive is to share the same cable, it should be set to Slave.

Most later PATA drives supported Cable Select (CS) which means the pin 28 connection in the cable will determine which drive is Master and which is Slave. New motherboards and drives ship with 80 wire ribbon cables which support cable select and feature the following color coded connectors: Motherboard IDE Connector - Blue, Slave IDE connector (middle connector on cable) - Grey, Master - Black. Cable Select is also supported by custom 40 wire ribbon cables and older

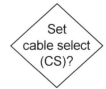

drives found in many brand-name systems. The jumpers on both drives should be set to cable select (CS) if you aren't setting one as Master and the other as Slave.

If the drives still don't register properly, make sure the power cable is seated in the drive's power socket, which can take a bit of force. The ribbon cable connectors must also be seated all the way into the IDE port on both the drives and the motherboard, or adapter card if you are using a RAID adapter. The most common reason for a cabling failure of this sort is that the connection was partially dislodged when you were working on something else in the case. Try a new ribbon cable. The most common cable failure is right at the connectors, which can break open if the locks fail. The connectors aren't soldered to the wires, the circuit is made mechanically with "V" shaped contacts forced through the plastic and digging into the conductors.

Are the ribbon cable connectors and the IDE ports on the drives and the motherboard keyed such that the cable can only go one way? Check the pin 1 location on all of the connectors and ports. On IDE drives, pin 1 is traditionally located next to the power socket, but it's not a 100% rule for all time. If the motherboard connector isn't boxed and keyed, it's possible to force the cable on backwards or miss an entire row of pins. The pin 1 location on the motherboard is normally marked with an arrow, a dot, a white square, anything to show one end of the interface as different from the other. If the motherboard won't register any drive you attach, even on new cables, and if those drives are spinning up, it indicates that either the IDE controller is bad or all the drives you've tried are bad. You can try running on the secondary IDE controller if you've only been working with the primary, but the next stop is installing an add-in IDE adapter or replacing the motherboard.

SMART is one of those cute acronyms you don't want to see popping up on your screen with a nasty message. Self-Monitoring, Analysis and Reporting Technology (SMART) is basically a predictor of doom, though it's up to you whether or not to heed it. Because the metrics defined include 87 different signals, from the spin-up time to the read-write error rate, to the drive temperature and vibrations, it's not fully implemented by every drive manufacturer in the same way.

Not all motherboards support SMART reporting, and it may be enabled or disabled in CMOS Setup. Operating system support for SMART is also sketchy, but you can find plenty of free downloadable monitoring tools that will run under any version of Windows and read the SMART information from the drive. If you do get a message warning of impending drive failure from the operating system or from the motherboard BIOS, it pays to back up your data and just replace the drive if you can afford it. Just don't fall for the malware that pretends to issue SMART. warnings!

The troubleshooting procedures for ATA interfaced drives that aren't recognized by the BIOS are identical, whether they are hard drives, CDs, DVDs, tapes or any other ATA device. If the BIOS registers the installed ATA drives correctly and the drive you're having problems with is a CD or DVD, proceed to the CD or DVD Failure diagnostics.

Solid State Drive (SSD) drive? Again, the troubleshooting tree branches for failure issues that affect mechanical drives vs. SSD drives. SSD drives will never spin up and spin down in an unending cycle because they don't spin, ever. Mechanical hard drives almost never require firmware updates, primarily because the operational parameters are fixed and there's not much that can be changed.

Does the drive cycle up and down? Try swapping the power lead for a spare or one used by another drive. For older IDE drives, try isolating the drive on its ribbon cable, even if it means temporarily doing without another drive for the sake of troubleshooting. If neither fix helps, try disconnecting the data cable to ensure that the drive isn't receiving some flaky power down signal from a bad ATA interface or a crazy power management scheme. If it still cycles up and down, the drive is likely toast. Test the drive in another system or a USB shell before labeling it dead.

If you have an old drive that spins up but won't seek (you never hear the head move in and out), it's probably a hardware failure. If you aren't sending the drive out for data recovery, one last ditch effort is tapping lightly with a screwdriver on the cover of the drive, away from the circular section where the platters are spinning. This might encourage a stuck head to get moving. A much debated "dead drive" hack is freezing the drive overnight (double freezer bag and desiccant), which may give you temporary access, before condensation or reheating causes failure. Make sure your backup media is ready if you try any last ditch efforts, because they likely won't work twice.

Does the drive make little clicking noises and fail to get going? The unending soft clicks are caused by the read/write head arm jerking back and forth in a series of seeks as it tries to read data from the platter. It could be that the magnetic coating is damaged, it could be tracking errors, it could be a variety of mechanical failures. Some data recovery technicians report receiving hard drives with randomly tightened cover screws (as a result of people trying to take them apart) which can cause clicking. If you own a quality torque screwdriver, it can't hurt to start on the lowest torque setting and see if some of the screws turn at low torques while others are tight. Restart the PC a couple times, and if you do get it booted, back up your data, run CHKDSK or ScanDisk, and try downloading a free utility that will let you check the drive's SMART report.

If you can't boot and you have data on the drive you want to recover, it always makes sense to try the drive as the second (non-boot) drive in another PC or to install it in a USB shell and hook it to a laptop. If the problem was in the boot sector and the drive indexing is undamaged, you may be able to read off all of your data. If not, you can try a 3rd party data recovery tool or send the drive out for data recovery if it's critical. If you don't mind losing all of the data onboard, you can try FDISKing and reinstalling the operating system again, but seek failures usually indicate the hardware is on its way out.

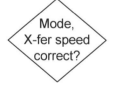

Does the BIOS report the transfer mode correctly for older PATA drives, like UDMA/100 or ATA/66? UDMA must be enabled in CMOS, or set on "Auto," for high speed transfers. You should never see any level of PIO selected for a hard drive. IDE hard drives manufactured after around 1995 require the 80 wire ribbon cable, at least for high speed operation. You can check CMOS Setup to see if there's a manual override to select the higher speed transfers, though the automatic settings should pick it up. Also try isolating the hard drive as the sole device on the primary controller. If you're adding a new hard drive to an older system, it's possible that the old motherboard and BIOS simply don't support the faster transfer, even with the new cable. I'd be leery of flashing the BIOS to try to get the speed up, even if the motherboard manufacturer supplies it.

Have you updated the firmware for your SSD drive? Unlike mechanical hard drives whose operational parameters are fixed, SSD drives sometimes benefit from new programming, but don't do it unless the manufacturer recommends the update. The SSD firmware controls the relatively high burden of housekeeping tasks that the SSD drive must perform independently of the PC, especially wear leveling and other tasks that will extend the life of the drive. Due to somewhat inconsistent operating system support, a firmware upgrade might be necessary after an automatic Windows update, or for compatibility with a particular high performance application.

Can you access the drive with any generation of Windows Disk Management or FDISK to view partitions? As long as the partition information is intact, the problem is more often malware or OS corruption than magnetic media or electronics failure. If the drive is loud but working, you should maintain up-to-date backups, but it may last for years. If the drive gets too hot, try repositioning it in the case so it can receive greater air flow, or add a case fan to the front of the case.

Does OS tool see drive?

If Windows is booted on this drive, make sure that the latest device drivers are installed for the motherboard, which include the integrated drive controller. If this is a secondary or external drive, check the drive partition in Disk Management to see whether it is allocated and "Healthy" as opposed to "Raw" and unallocated. For other hard drive issues, proceed to the Hard Drive Boot and Performance troubleshooting flowchart.

Hard Drive Boot and Performance

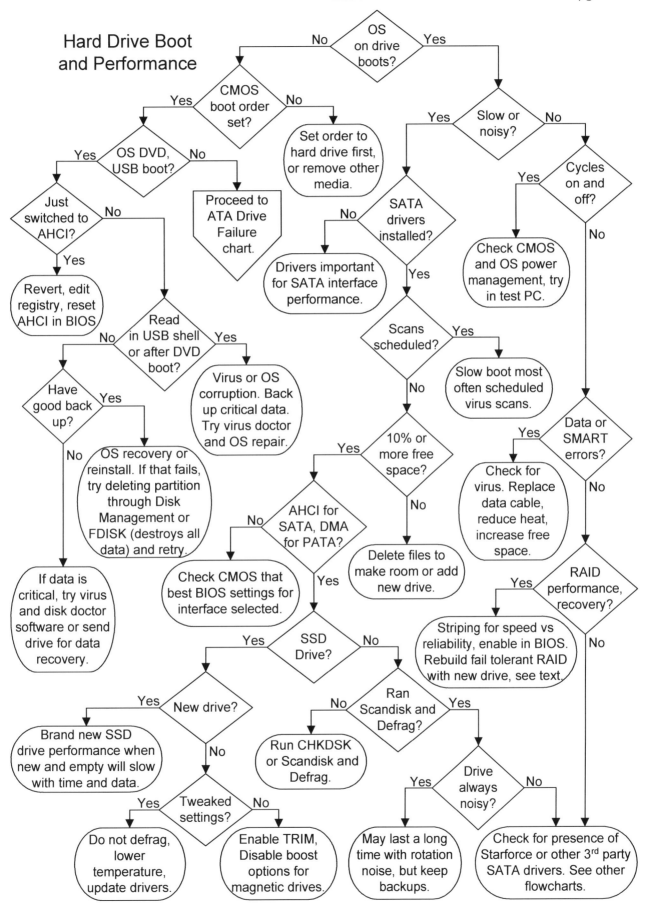

OS on drive boots?

No → CMOS boot order set?

Yes → OS DVD, USB boot?

Yes → Just switched to AHCI?

Yes → Revert, edit registry, reset AHCI in BIOS

No → Read in USB shell or after DVD boot?

No → Have good back up?

Yes → OS recovery or reinstall. If that fails, try deleting partition through Disk Management or FDISK (destroys all data) and retry.

No → If data is critical, try virus and disk doctor software or send drive for data recovery.

Yes → Virus or OS corruption. Back up critical data. Try virus doctor and OS repair.

No → Proceed to ATA Drive Failure chart.

No → Set order to hard drive first, or remove other media.

Yes → Slow or noisy?

Yes → SATA drivers installed?

No → Drivers important for SATA interface performance.

Yes → Scans scheduled?

Yes → Slow boot most often scheduled virus scans.

No → 10% or more free space?

Yes → AHCI for SATA, DMA for PATA?

No → Check CMOS that best BIOS settings for interface selected.

Yes → SSD Drive?

Yes → New drive?

Yes → Brand new SSD drive performance when new and empty will slow with time and data.

No → Tweaked settings?

Yes → Do not defrag, lower temperature, update drivers.

No → Enable TRIM, Disable boost options for magnetic drives.

No → Ran Scandisk and Defrag?

No → Run CHKDSK or Scandisk and Defrag.

Yes → Drive always noisy?

Yes → May last a long time with rotation noise, but keep backups.

No → Check for presence of Starforce or other 3rd party SATA drivers. See other flowcharts.

No → Delete files to make room or add new drive.

No → Cycles on and off?

Yes → Check CMOS and OS power management, try in test PC.

No → Data or SMART errors?

Yes → Check for virus. Replace data cable, reduce heat, increase free space.

No → RAID performance, recovery?

Yes → Striping for speed vs reliability, enable in BIOS. Rebuild fail tolerant RAID with new drive, see text.

Hard Drive Boot and Performance

Do you get at least a partial operating system load on a boot drive? This includes the Windows splash screen, or even just the running dots when a kernel is loading. Has the drive been moved from another system? Try booting in Safe Mode, since all the drivers for the underlying hardware will be incorrect in Windows. It's possible for a drive that's been moved from another system to begin booting even if the drive parameters and addressing mode have been detected incorrectly. Old PCs accepted manual input of hard drive parameters that can't always be auto-detected by a new motherboard. Otherwise, boot failure may be unrelated to the drive itself and due to a hardware conflict, data corruption, a bad install, etc. If your performance issue is with a second (non-boot) hard drive, follow the "Yes" branch of the flowchart.

Have you checked the boot order of all the installed devices in CMOS Setup? The boot order specifies which drive should be tried first and should be set to your boot hard drive unless you are having trouble with an operating system install. Boot order problems come up quite frequently these days since practically all newer PCs support booting from a USB storage device, a memory stick or an SSD. If the boot order is set to USB and anything that can be interpreted as a drive is attached, including the memory card of a camera left in a digital film reader, the BIOS may try to boot it and simply lock up rather than going on to the next device. If you absolutely prefer to leave USB or the DVD as the first boot device, unplug any USB attached devices and remove any media from those drives. If the hard drive still fails to boot, set it to be the first boot device and try again.

Can you boot from a bootable USB memory stick, SSD or from an operating system DVD or CD? If not, this is where you change the boot order to try the USB device or the DVD first. The USB test isn't perfect because if you've never tried booting a USB device on the PC before, the BIOS support may not be 100%. You should use a USB port on the back of the PC (in the motherboard I/O core) rather than a front mounted USB port, which may be slower or shared. Likewise, if you are trying to boot an operating system DVD or an old CD, it could be that the CD/DVD drive is taking too long to spin up and the BIOS is timing out. Try ejecting the disc, hitting the reset button on the PC, and then sliding the tray back in so that the drive will be

spinning up by itself by the time the BIOS checks for a CD. Confirm that the DVD is bootable in another PC, try wiping it off with a flannel shirt if it's covered with finger prints.

If you can boot from a USB device, but not from a hard drive with a known good operating system installed or a bootable operating system DVD, it sounds like an ATA controller or cabling problem and you need to return to the ATA Failure chart. If you can't boot from a USB device or a DVD when the PC has done so in the past, it's more likely a motherboard failure issue, so see the Motherboard, CPU and RAM chart.

Have you just switched to AHCI in CMOS Setup to boost the performance for your SATA hard drive or SSD? AHCI (Advance Host Controller Interface) is an Intel created standard that allows SATA devices to perform at their best, rather than being limited by a BIOS that only understands the older IDE devices and basically runs the SATA devices in compatibility mode. But switching to AHCI after the operating system has already been installed on the boot drive can lead to boot failure. The reason is that some Windows releases that support SATA (Windows Vista and Windows 7) don't install the AHCI drivers unless AHCI is enabled in the BIOS before the operating system install.

If you have this problem, it's too late to tell you that you should have enabled AHCI first, but it's not too late to make the switch. You will have to revert to the original BIOS setting in order to get the PC booted, and then you'll have to install any required motherboard drivers for the SATA controller in Windows and edit the registry entry. This varies with the operating system version and service pack, so do an Internet search for exact instructions with screen shots. After you've made all of the required changes, you can re-enable AHCI in the BIOS in CMOS Setup and reboot.

After you've booted from a USB device or an operating system DVD, can you exit to the command line and read the information on the hard drive that failed to boot? Can you read the hard drive data if it's installed in an external USB shell? If you can, it's likely the operating system has been corrupted. This could be due to a virus, an actual error writing to the hard drive, or a piece of software running amok and writing data to the wrong location on the drive. Back up any critical data while you can access the drive, then try running ScanDisk, CHKDSK or an equivalent and see if it can repair the drive. Otherwise, you can try to use the Windows DVD to repair or reinstall (options depend on particular OS and PC manufacturer). Most operating systems allow you to reinstall without wiping out any of your data or programs. They (should) always prompt you to see if you want to continue before actually destroying any data. But if the hard drive was making a repeated clicking sound when it tried to boot, there's a good chance there is physical damage in the boot sector, and getting the data off is the best you can hope for.

Do you have a good backup? A good backup doesn't just mean that you've plugged in an external hard drive that's supposed to handle automatic back-ups, it means that you've actually checked the external hard drive to make sure that the files you need are on there and that you can access them. Internet back-up services are actually more reliable than local back-ups, and if you only care about a small number of files, like the novel you are writing, e-mailing it as an attachment to your Yahoo!, Hotmail or Gmail account is all that it takes. If you do have a good backup and the OS recovery has failed, you can try deleting the partitions on the drive through Windows Disk Management or FDISK and starting from scratch. This means losing all of the information on your drive, so if you have any critical data and you aren't sure of what you're doing, seek professional help.

If you don't have a good backup and the data is critical, you might want to invest in the latest disk doctor and virus doctor software you can find. If the data is going-out-of-business critical, you can send the drive out to a data recovery outfit. Data recovery is expensive, from the mid-hundreds to thousands of dollars, but they can usually recover data from a drive as long as it hasn't been maliciously wiped out and the data platters haven't been physically damaged. Unfortunately, data recovery from SSD drives is more difficult as SSD drives are subject to catastrophic software control failures and the information on the chip level is not organized as simply as the data on magnetic hard drives.

Is the drive slow, meaning slower than it used to be or slower than you expected based on experience? Is the drive noisy, either in terms of volume ("That's one loud drive") or simply because it never stops seeking? You can download test software from the Internet that will report on hard drive performance through read/write tests and can turn up problems with the interface or BIOS settings, but hardware testing won't tell you anything about the presence of malware or data fragmentation. If the hard drive status LED on the front of the computer blinks

continually after the operating system has finished loading and before you've begun working, count that as "slow."

Can you actually hear the drive spinning up whenever you do something that requires drive access? If you have an SSD hard drive, you must be hearing fan noise from the power supply or a heatsink fan because the drive has no mechanical parts. When "regular" hard drives cycle up and down, it either indicates a bad power supply, bad instructions from the controller, or that the drive is failing.

You can eliminate bad instructions from the controller by simply disconnecting the data cable and seeing if the cycling stops. Obviously, the system won't be able to boot during this test and you'll probably see a "hard drive failure" message. It could just be that the power management settings for the drive are too aggressive and that either the operating system or the BIOS (through CMOS Setup) is telling the hard drive to power down any time you don't access it for 60 seconds. Turn off power management in CMOS Setup, at least for the hard drive, if that's an option. Check the power management settings in Windows Control Panel and turn off hard drive power management.

If the hard drive cycles up and down even without the data cable connected, it's either the power supply or failing drive electronics. Try a different power supply lead to the drive, and if that doesn't help, test the hard drive in another PC or in an external powered USB cage to see if it still cycles up and down before giving up. Since the failure is with the drive electronics, it's a good candidate to send out for data recovery if you have critical data that isn't backed up.

SMART (Self-Monitoring, Analysis and Reporting Technology) has been around forever and it's generally implemented well by hard drive manufacturers. But it's not always supported by the motherboard BIOS, and is often disabled in the BIOS by default even when it is supported. SMART tracks dozens of hard drive operational parameters, error counts, temperatures, etc, which can be accessed through the operating system if you download a free testing program that includes SMART data. The hard drive manufacturers all supply free hard drive diagnostic software on their websites, but for their brand of drive only. When SMART is implemented properly through the BIOS, you'll get a warning of impending failure when the error counts reach a pre-defined critical point for the drive. If you get a legitimate SMART error message from the BIOS, it's time to back up critical data and replace the drive.

Hard drive data errors can manifest as error messages from the BIOS that specify HDD errors, they can show up when running ScanDisk or CHKDSK, or they can cause BSOD (Blue Screen Of Death) errors, commonly followed by a Windows message on the next boot-up that the system was shut down improperly and a scan to test data integrity is required. Newer hard drives all have the built-in ability to transparently manage a reasonable number of magnetic media failures by moving around data and closing off bad sectors on the drive, so when errors are serious enough to report, it's worth taking notice.

Does your drive accumulate data errors over time? Have you had to reinstall the operating system more than once, or is CHKDSK or ScanDisk constantly telling you that it's recovering lost files? Try downloading and running the hard drive manufacturer's diagnostic software, or on older PCs, running a "Thorough" scan with ScanDisk, which verifies the physical disk surfaces and can take all night on a large hard drive. If physical errors on the drive are identified and repaired (the software marks them as bad and removes them from use), and new errors are discovered the next time you run the test, the drive is failing.

As always, check the IDE or SATA data cable, and if you've been fooling around in the case quite a bit, it's worth a shot to replace it. Check for viruses. Errors can result from the drive running too hot, so if it's a hundred degrees in the room, consider air conditioning or moving the PC. It can also get pretty hot in the case even in an air-conditioned environment if there isn't enough air circulation in the case and the drives are stacked in like pancakes. RF interference on the data cable is another (remote) possibility, caused by a poorly designed or partially failed adapter on the bus that's acting like a broadcast antenna at just the wrong frequency and overwhelms error correction. Back up all of your data (really the first thing you should do when you start seeing data errors on a drive) and reformat the drive. Do a slow format, not the fast format some OS installs allow. You know it's a slow format when it takes hours.

The most common RAID implementation these days is RAID 0, which is strictly for performance. If you had two drives installed in your PC for the sake of data security, then you are probably running a RAID 1 array. RAID 1 mirrors every bit of data on both drives, so if one drive fails, the system should inform you

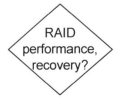

RAID performance, recovery?

that it needs to be replaced but continue running as usual. The problem is, many people confuse drive integrity with data security. If you get a virus or other malware infestation, or if you accidentally delete data, the deletion or infestation is mirrored to both drives. The only true security is in incrementally backing up your data and storing multiple copies offsite.

If you have three or more hard drives installed in a server, you're probably running a RAID 5 configuration. RAID 5 employs both data striping and parity (a form of error checking) so that in the case of a single drive failure, the array can rebuild itself with no data loss when the failed drive is replaced with an empty new drive. If you've reached this point without finding your hard drive performance issue, it's likely a software problem (some copy protection software can slow drive performance) or an OS compatibility problem with the controller.

Have you installed the SATA drivers that came with the motherboard and updated the SATA drivers to the latest version? Many home builders skip this step in their eagerness to get the system up and running, and they never know the difference (except in performance) because the BIOS can manage the interface between the SATA controller and Windows without the drivers, it just doesn't do as good a job of it. Performance is strongly dependent on efficient communications between the SATA controller and the operating system, and that's why the drivers are needed.

The #1 reason for slow boot times followed by slower than normal performance for the first half hour or so of operation is that a virus scan is running in the background. Don't launch any programs after starting the PC, just wait for the hard drive activity LED to stop. If the hard drive LED is still indicating heavy usage five minutes and fifteen minutes after boot, it usually means that virus software is running a full scan on start-up. This happens when the virus software is set to scan the PC on boot, or the scan is scheduled for the middle of the night (when the PC is powered down) and the software tries to catch up on its schedule the next time the PC is powered up.

First make sure the drive isn't getting too full. My rule of thumb, used to be keeping 20% free space on a drive for temporary files and the Windows swap file, but the drives have gotten so big that 10% is probably enough. Many programs create large temporary files without really documenting the fact, so you can be sure you always need more free space than you think. When you delete files and directories to free up space on the drive, you also have to empty your Windows trash, or the space doesn't actually become available. The main culprits are downloaded music and videos. It would take ten thousand Shakespeares writing for a thousand years to fill up a hard drive with text.

Have you checked the BIOS selections for the hard drive controller in CMOS Setup? SATA drives should use AHCI (Advanced Host Controller Interface) unless the BIOS doesn't support it, but if AHCI isn't selected, see the decision point for "Just switched to AHCI?" before taking action. Parallel ATA (IDE) controllers should be set for the fastest DMA or UDMA mode supported, and never for PIO. You should also check older versions of Windows for the hard drive interface mode if you had some hard drive errors after which Windows slowed to a crawl. Some Windows versions would automatically revert to PIO after a number of hard drive time-outs. This problem is more common with secondary drives than the boot drive, but it can happen with any PATA device, including DVD and CD drives. If you search the Internet for "DMA reverts to PIO" you'll find some free tools that will save you from having to edit the registry if that's not in your comfort zone.

Is the drive with performance issues an SSD? Both SSD and mechanical drives share a number of performance troubleshooting steps associated with the operating system and these were addressed above. But the underlying technology differences between SSD and magnetic hard drives means the final troubleshooting steps diverge. For example, you never want to run DEFRAG on an SSD.

Have you defragmented the disk recently? Run Defrag by right clicking the drive in My Computer, choosing Properties and then Tools (in older Windows versions, this is found under Programs > Accessories > System Tools). If Defrag gives you any grief, try running CHKDSK or ScanDisk first. Some Windows versions also have a tool called System File Checker which runs as the Admin command: "sfc /scannow" for which Microsoft offers a tutorial on their website.

If CHKDSK or ScanDisk doesn't make it all the way through the drive, make sure you aren't running any other programs (you can often use ctrl-alt-del to end all the non-critical tasks), and try again. If it still doesn't work, restart in Safe Mode and try. If you still can't get through ScanDisk, consider backing up your data and reformatting the drive. It's a tough call at this point, if you've defragged the drive, it's not full, and it's still slowly beating itself to death. Buy or download some decent virus doctor and spyware eradicator software, because you probably have a virus or a mess of spyware on the drive making life miserable.

If your drive is continually noisy, sounds like a quiet airplane as it spins up and then makes high pitched rotational noise all the time, it's just mechanical noise. While it's not a good sign, and I would suggest replacing the drive, I've also seen noisy hard drives linger for years and years. If the drive starts sounding like a penny rattling around in a tin can, it's time to back up your data, but if it's sounded that way for years, it's just poorly built. Make sure there are four screws securing the drive in both cases.

If there were no physical symptoms or signs of error, and the drive diagnostics software didn't turn anything up, it's possible that a third party driver is interfering with hard drive performance. Some gamers report that the Starforce copy protection scheme for games, at least in some versions, uses drivers that can degrade drive performance. So check the user forums for the game software installed on your PC and see if there are known issues. Otherwise, it's possible that the performance bottleneck you are experiencing with the hard drive is really due to a different hardware issue, so check the other flowcharts.

Is your SSD brand new? Some home builders and upgraders add an SSD for use with games or to replace their boot drive and immediately start running performance tests to see what they got for their money. The problem is that SSD drive performance can degrade rapidly in the first few hours and weeks of use as the drive fills up. This isn't a failure a failure as long as the performance stops degrading at a level that's equal to or higher than advertised.

There are several figures of merit used for specifying SSD performance, but I like using MB/s for apples-to-apples comparison with standard hard drives. For starters, keep in mind that the fastest standard interface for hard drives, SATA 3, has a maximum transfer rate of around 600 MB/s, but the best mechanical hard drives rarely manage 100 MB/s, unless the data happens to be in cache.

Rates of 600 MB/s and higher are possible with SSDs, though currently, the only drives capable of rates above the SATA 3 maximum are found in servers using Serial SCSI or FibreChannel interfaces. You may see your SSD rated in IOPS, Input/Output Operations Per Second, which can actually be translated into MB/s if you know the size of the test transfer in bytes. When rated in IOPS, high performance magnetic hard drives (10,000 rpm) on an SATA 3 interface can achieve ratings as high as 150 IOPS and Serial Attached SCSI drives for servers can break 200 IOPS. The IOPS ratings for SSD drives are at least an order of magnitude higher, in the thousands or tens of thousands (higher for server drives). But the IOPS metric favors SSDs for their random access ability, the transfer rate for large amounts of data is not always that much higher in PC applications, sometimes as low as 100 MB/s.

Have you tweaked the Windows and BIOS settings for your particular SSD? SSD drives are relatively new, so both manufacturers and gamers are still determining how to get the most out of them. Certainly you should disable any scheduled drive maintenance tasks in Windows (especially DEFRAG), and disable Indexing under the properties tab for the SSD. Other suggestions range from disabling Windows write-back cache to enabling disk data cache. You should also make sure that TRIM is enabled (TRIM is a command, not an acronym) in Windows 7 and later versions. Some experts will suggest you disable System Restore, but that means losing the ability easily cure many simple malware and accidental registry corruption issues.

If you've tried performance tweaks in software settings and you still aren't happy with the transfer rate, make doubly sure you have all of the drivers for the SSD and the SATA controller installed. And although SATA cables aren't always rated for speed, if your SATA 3 SSD is on an SATA 3 controller, make sure the cable is rated for 6 Gb/s. Check the SSD manufacturer website to see if they recommend a firmware update, remembering that a failed firmware update can leave you with nothing. See also the Motherboard, CPU and RAM Performance diagnostics in case the problem is really slow overall performance and not the fault of the SSD.

DVD, CD and
Blu-Ray Playback

DVD, CD and Blu-ray Playback

The most basic and potentially most disastrous problem that can occur with an optical drive is a stuck tray. Will the tray eject when you press the eject button? Press it once, like a doorbell, and then move your finger away, or you may be sending it repeated open and close commands. The drive won't pop right open if it is actively playing a disc, and the operating system may be able to override the stop and open command. If you're trying to eject a music CD or DVD using Media Player software (clicking on a software eject button on the screen) and it doesn't work, try the manual button on the drive. If this is a newly installed drive, make sure you used the short screws shipped with the drive and not longer screws which can jam the mechanism. If there's a disc in the drive that can no longer be read, make sure the power supply lead is still seated in the socket on the back of the drive.

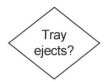

Shut down, restart, and try again. If the tray still doesn't eject, reboot again and note whether the BIOS registers the drive. Some brand name PCs don't report installed hardware on a boot screen, so you'll have to access CMOS Setup to check. If the BIOS doesn't register the drive, it may have dropped dead. Proceed to ATA Drive Failure if the BIOS no longer registers the drive.

Before you start tearing apart the machine, make sure that the tray isn't locked by software. The drawer will not eject while the drive is busy. If the operating system driver works properly, the hardware eject button will interrupt whatever software is controlling the drive. The easiest way to check if software is preventing a manual eject is to reboot the PC and hit the eject button before the operating system loads. You can also check the properties under the drive icon in Windows "My Computer." Some media player software may lock the hardware eject button, but you can eject using the software eject button on the player if everything is working.

Assuming the drive is still registered by the BIOS and seen by the operating system, you really do have a stuck disc. The next step is to look for a pinhole on the front of the CD or DVD drive. Power down the system and unplug the power cord, then straighten out a couple inches worth of paper clip, the heaviest gauge that will fit in the hole. Gently push the paper clip straight into the hole until you feel it depress the release mechanism.

This will often cause the tray to pop out a fraction of an inch, other times you will have to pry it a little to get it started. Once you have enough tray sticking out to grab it with your fingers, you should be able to pull it out far enough to remove the disc. If the faceplate seems to be bulging as you pull, the disc is hung up on it, and the best thing to do is remove the drive from the PC and then remove the faceplate.

If you still can't get the tray to eject and you need to recover the disc, the only option is to disassemble the drive. The odds of the drive being repairable are low because ejection failures are due to a broken mechanism for which you are unlikely to find replacement parts at less than the cost of a new drive.

Does the drive cause the whole PC to tremble when it spins up? Is it noisy? Make sure that the drive is mounted with four screws, and level. High speed drives will vibrate like crazy if a disc is off balance, usually because the disc itself has some weighting problem. Aside from obvious physical flaws (like the dog or the kid took a bite out of the edge of the disc) a miss-applied label can create an unbalanced disc. Try ejecting and reinserting the disc. Don't keep running a drive that vibrates badly even if it plays discs. It could end up damaging the discs (discs have been known to shatter at high speeds) and it doesn't do the other components in your system any good to be vibrated, which can lead to connections working apart or worse. If the problem only occurs with some discs, you can blame the discs. Otherwise, purchase a new drive.

Does your problem involve recording DVDs, CDs or Blu-ray discs? If so, proceed to the Recording Problems flowchart. For a problem playing or booting a factory CD in a recorder, stay here. It's become increasingly difficult to tell factory pressed CDs from recorded CDs, due to the highly polished labels that can be easily printed for recorded CDs and DVDs. Factory produced discs are usually silver on the read surface, while recorded discs are often gold or green, or show two different tones of silver.

Does the drive read discs? When you mount a disc, be it software or music, does the drive acknowledge that a disc is present and let you view the contents? It doesn't matter (at this point) whether or not you can get through installing the software on the disc or playing the movie or music. The question is simply, can the drive see anything at all on the disc?

Is the problem with a Blu-ray drive? The Blu-ray standard has not caught on with PC manufacturers in a big way, and one of the results is that the software support is sketchy. When new operating systems and software appear, the drive may not only require a new driver, but also a firmware update from the drive manufacturer. Other than checking for a firmware update, the troubleshooting for Blu-ray drives follows the same path as that for DVD drives.

Does the drive play CDs but not DVDs or DVDs but not CDs? Can it play Blu-ray but not DVDs, or any other mix-and-match combination? The different generations of optical discs are read by different color lasers (different wavelengths of light) through different lenses. Manufacturers played some pretty clever tricks in making DVD drives backwards compatible with CDs using a single laser, but some designs include multiple lasers or mechanically swapped lenses. This means is it's possible for a laser failure or one dirty lens to lead to a drive that can play one generation of media and not another. Confirm this with multiple factory discs and try cleaning before replacing the drive.

Can you listen to music CDs through your speakers? The following assumes that you can get operating system sounds to play from your speakers. If not, proceed to Sound Failure. First, make sure that the CD isn't muted in the software mixer panel. Next, if the drive is equipped with an audio jack on the front, stick in a cheap headphone (if you have one) and see if the CD is playing. In any case, if the CD is spinning and the time is advancing in whatever version of Media Player you have installed, the drive is actually playing the CD. New drives support DAE (Digital Audio Extraction) and some SATA drives don't support the old analog audio output at all. If you have a newer drive, check the DAE settings in the drive properties.

Older drives, both SATA and PATA (IDE), required an analog patch cord inside the case. The audio patch cord from the drive to the sound card or the sound port on the motherboard may not be connected, or the device volume could be turned down in a software mixer panel. The easy check for an incorrect audio patch cable (3 or 4 wires) connection without opening the PC is to try a multimedia disc, such as a game, because sound coded in the game software bypasses the direct D/A (Digital to Analog) conversion of music CDs. Note also that in two drive systems, the builder may only have patched the audio output of one of the drives through to the sound card.

Illustrated drive replacement:

www.fonerbooks.com /r_cd.htm

If you can't play movies in your DVD that you can play on a television DVD player, the problem is usually with the software CODEC (COder/DECoder). Test the movie on a TV player first to make sure the disc is good. The media player you are using may display a specific error message, like telling you the screen properties must be set to a certain resolution and number of colors for a movie to play. Or, the player may report that it can't find a decoder (CODEC) to play the particular disc. Even if the movie worked last night, your media player may have received an automated update the next time you went online that rendered the installed CODEC obsolete.

If you search the Internet, you'll find plenty of people trying to sell you CODECs, but if you stay away from the advertisements, you should be able to find the updated version for free. You may also encounter new copy protection schemes that render some discs unplayable on your PC even though you aren't trying to copy them. The only solution for this again lays in software and Internet research for the specific failure. It may turn out that the only way to render your DVD player compatible with a new type of copy protection is to update the DVD drive firmware. If an update isn't available for your particular model, you can end up out of luck when it comes to playing discs from certain studios after a particular date.

Does your system refuse to boot bootable factory DVDs or CDs, like operating systems from the last fifteen years? Try setting the boot sequence in CMOS Setup to boot to the optical drive first. While this shouldn't really be necessary for new builds if the hard drive is uninitiated, it often fixes the problem. Some older high speed drives take too long to spin up and report to the BIOS that there's a bootable disc present. Sometimes you can get around this by opening and closing the tray, which should cause the drive to spin up, and hitting reset right after you've done so. With any luck, you'll get the timing right so that the BIOS checks for a bootable disc while the drive is still active. Make sure you test the boot disc in another PC, and if you are trying to get by with a recorded boot disc, at least test it in a different PC than the one where it was recorded.

If your drive reads data, plays movies and music, boots bootable discs, and doesn't vibrate or make noise, it's likely a PC performance problem is degrading the playback. Try ending other programs, and use the Widows performance monitor to see if your CPU and memory usage are swamped.

Do you have Blu-ray and DVD drives installed? It's easy enough to mix up drives on a PC, and a DVD drive isn't going to going to have much luck reading a Blu-ray disc. A CD recorder along with a DVD player was a common two drive combination years ago, but the DVD may not be able to read CDs recorded just two inches away. Check the drive for compatibility logos, Blu-ray drives may not be fully backwards compatible. See Recording Problems if you're having trouble reading a recorded disc. Some ancient systems have both a CD ROM (reader) and a CDR (recorder).

Are you reading the right drive? If you have two physical drives, make sure the operating system is actually looking at the drive the disc has been placed in. Trust me, I've been fooled myself into opening up a machine by blind belief in the wrong drive letter, and just a couple months ago I was called in to look at a drive failure in a two drive system where the owner had labeled them incorrectly with stickers. Most drives have an activity LED that tells you when the drive is active. Make sure the activity LED is lighting up on the drive you put the disc in when you try to read it.

Does the drive read other discs? Try another factory disc if you've been having trouble with recorded discs. If the factory disc works, the issue is with the media or drive compatibility, and it's unlikely any tweaks will cure that. Clean the disc with a soft bit of flannel. The discs are plastic, so don't use solvents. Scratches can render a disc unreadable, including deep scratches on the label surface which cause distortions in the layer that is actually being read from the bottom. Try the disc in another reader before chucking it out, it could just have trouble with the device you were trying it in.

Have you run a lens cleaner disc? Laser lens cleaning discs are purpose built for cleaning optical drives. They cost around $10 through a retail store, cheaper if you buy them online through third parties. The discs clean the lenses by physical contact, running brushes over them as the drive spins the disc. A surprising number of reviewers on sites like Amazon report that a cleaning disc fixed their problem. Since the disc will be rotating at high speed in the drive, do not try to improve the process by adding isopropyl alcohol to the brushes, because the centrifugal effect will just splatter it on the electronics.

Does the drive fail to show up in My Computer on your desktop, or is it flagged with an error in Device Manager? The first step is to reinstall the driver. Delete the drive in Device Manager, reboot, and let Windows reinstall it. If you can boot an operating system disc in the drive, but the drive doesn't appear in Device Manager, the drive is being handled properly by the BIOS but not Windows. Make sure your virus software is functioning and download and run the latest comprehensive malware checker with good ratings since some malware interferes with the optical drive. Check if there's a firmware update for the drive itself on the manufacturer's website.

If you're using a newer SATA DVD recorder/player or a Blu-ray, there aren't any jumpers to set or cable sharing issues. If it's a new build, make sure that you don't have the data cable attached to a dedicated SATA RAID controller. But the safest way to determine if there's a problem with your SATA cable, or a compatibility issue with the BIOS, is to try the drive in another PC, or mount it in a powered 5.25" USB shell and connect it externally.

If you are using an old IDE drive, it could have a simple cabling problem or Master/Slave conflict. If the drive is the Slave on primary IDE controller with the hard drive, move it to the secondary IDE controller as the Master (requires another IDE ribbon cable). If you already have another device installed as the secondary Master, try the drive as the secondary Slave or temporarily replace the Master for the sake of seeing if it works.

Did the drive test out as working when you tried it in an external USB shell or in another PC? If so, the problem is either with your motherboard controller and drivers, or a hardware incompatibility.

If the drive fails to work in another PC or running in an external USB cage, the hardware is at fault. Before replacing the drive, you can take it apart and try manually cleaning the laser lens with a Q-tip and some isopropyl alcohol. It usually means removing the bottom surface of the drive, followed by the wrap-around shell, and then removing a circuit board to gain access. Be careful with any ribbon cables, since they aren't made for rough handling. You can find many decent video tutorials for this on YouTube.

DVD, Blu-Ray and CD Recording Problems

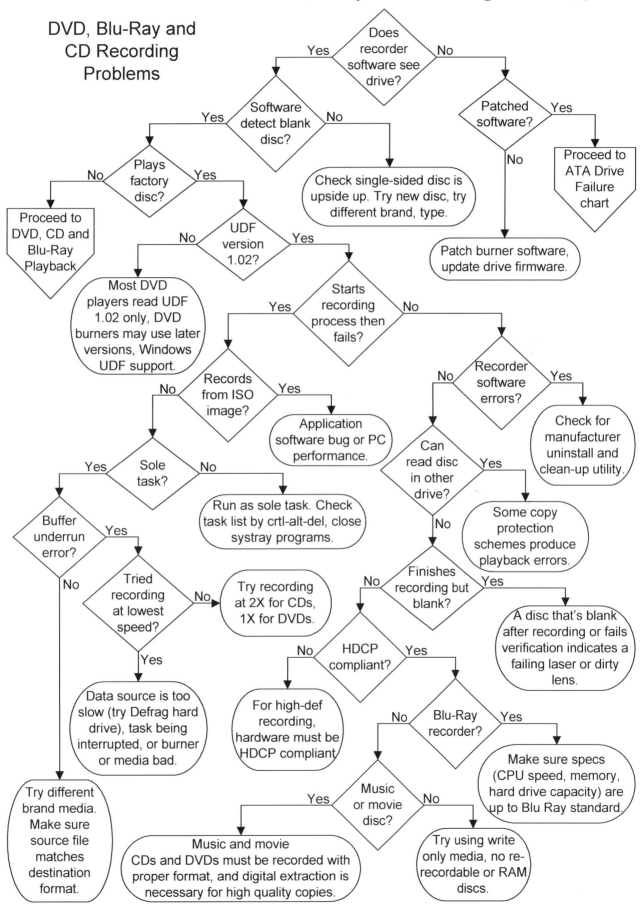

Does recorder software see drive?

Yes → Software detect blank disc?

No → Patched software?

Yes → Proceed to ATA Drive Failure chart

No → Patch burner software, update drive firmware.

Software detect blank disc?

Yes → Plays factory disc?

No → Check single-sided disc is upside up. Try new disc, try different brand, type.

Plays factory disc?

No → Proceed to DVD, CD and Blu-Ray Playback

Yes → UDF version 1.02?

UDF version 1.02?

No → Most DVD players read UDF 1.02 only, DVD burners may use later versions, Windows UDF support.

Yes → Starts recording process then fails?

Starts recording process then fails?

Yes → Records from ISO image?

No → Recorder software errors?

Recorder software errors?

Yes → Check for manufacturer uninstall and clean-up utility.

No → Can read disc in other drive?

Records from ISO image?

No → Sole task?

Yes → Application software bug or PC performance.

Can read disc in other drive?

Yes → Some copy protection schemes produce playback errors.

No → Finishes recording but blank?

Sole task?

Yes → Buffer underrun error?

No → Run as sole task. Check task list by crtl-alt-del, close systray programs.

Finishes recording but blank?

No → HDCP compliant?

Yes → A disc that's blank after recording or fails verification indicates a failing laser or dirty lens.

Buffer underrun error?

Yes → Tried recording at lowest speed?

No → Try different brand media. Make sure source file matches destination format.

Tried recording at lowest speed?

No → Try recording at 2X for CDs, 1X for DVDs.

Yes → Data source is too slow (try Defrag hard drive), task being interrupted, or burner or media bad.

HDCP compliant?

No → For high-def recording, hardware must be HDCP compliant

Yes → Blu-Ray recorder?

Blu-Ray recorder?

Yes → Make sure specs (CPU speed, memory, hard drive capacity) are up to Blu Ray standard.

No → Music or movie disc?

Music or movie disc?

Yes → Music and movie CDs and DVDs must be recorded with proper format, and digital extraction is necessary for high quality copies.

No → Try using write only media, no re-recordable or RAM discs.

Recording Problem DVD, CD, Blu-ray

Does the recorder software, whether the native operating system software or a third party recording suite, see the burner and correctly identify it? It doesn't matter if you can play a DVD or music CD in the drive, that basic level of compatibility is ensured by the BIOS providing the drive isn't dead and is connected right. Get the latest version of the driver from the recorder manufacturer's web site.

Even though recording software was probably bundled with your drive or PC when you bought it, that doesn't necessarily mean the software is up-to-date for your particular model or the operating system release you're running. If your drive was sold with OEM software, rather than a full version, and an update for your drive isn't available, it's possible that software won't work with the drive at all and you may be stuck buying a retail version of the software. When it comes to software compatibility, start by checking the drive manufacturer's web site to see if they have a firmware upgrade for the recorder. Next, check the burner software website and see if they have a patch for recognizing the particular make and model of your drive. If none of the software updates allow the recording software to see the drive, you'll have to try a different drive or different recording software. But if the drive doesn't even show up in the BIOS, see the ATA Drive Failure flowchart.

Does the recorder software detect that a recordable disc is in the drive? The most common error when using cheap discs sold without any labeling is mounting them in the drive tray upside down. You can try turning the disc over, or if there are numbers printed around the spindle hole in the center of the disc, the disc is upside up when you can read them. Try cleaning the disc. It may be bad, even if it looks perfectly good to the eye (no scratches, fingerprints, etc). I've seen failure rates as high as 20% or more with brand name discs that have been sitting around for a while. Make sure the disc type you purchased is compatible with your recorder.

Can you play a factory disc, whether a movie, music disc, or retail purchased software? Try several different discs if the first one fails, and you might want to give a laser cleaning disc (around $10) a chance. If the drive won't play any discs, see the DVD, CD and Blu-ray Playback flowchart.

Is the UDF (Universal Disc Format) 1.02 version supported by the drive and software? This was an especially common problem with Windows XP and certain recorders. Recorded discs that use a UDF standard newer than 1.02 may only work if the older ISO format is chosen when recording, or they may not work at all. If the software gives the option, you should burn UDP 1.02 for maximum compatibility. In some cases, downloading newer UDF support for the operating system may help read newer discs.

Does your recorder begin the recording process, and then fail? Note that this renders the "write only" or "R" as in CDR or DVDR media useless. Some people like using the rewriteable media to test that recording will work before using a write only blank, especially with more expensive Blu-ray blanks, but so many problems are media specific that you'll eventually have to gamble on a write-only disc. Make a note of where the recording process halts, percentage wise. If it always fails at the same point, there's a very good chance the problem is with a particular file that's needed at that point which can't be accessed.

Does the burn session succeed if you write an image file to the hard drive and record from that? Whether your recording session fails from within a software application or while burning from a file list in the native recorder software, the first test to try is to create an image file on the hard drive. The image file, often referred to as an ISO image, eliminates the possibility that the recording is failing because the required file elements aren't available or can't be accessed quickly enough. If you can burn a disc from the image file, the problem is probably in the software application (especially if it's within an editing suite or rendering program), but it's also possible your overall PC performance is just too slow while running the application. If you can't even write an image file, the problem is definitely with the software or operating system settings.

Close all other tasks so that the recording process is the only job your PC is working on. Other tasks can include work you are doing in another program, as well as background tasks running on the Internet. There are various 3rd party software packages capable of controlling background tasks, but you can usually get by with ctrl-alt-del and the Windows Task List, once you get a feel for which tasks are superfluous to what you're doing. It's also possible that the recorder is kaput. After you eliminate media as a problem by trying different discs, test the recorder in another machine with all of the latest software (both drivers and burner software) before giving up on it.

If you get a buffer underrun error, it means the recorder has run out of data to write to the disc continually and fails. Newer recorders and software with buffer underrun protection that allows them to restart recording without a gap in the track shouldn't have this problem. Try defragging the hard drive before you record discs, and if the defrag utility keeps restarting, it's usually a sign that some other task is competing with it for the hard drive's attention. Make sure your virus suite isn't running a full system scan in the background.

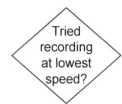

Check if the drive can successfully record discs to completion at a lower speed. Try the lowest speed possible, which depends on both the recorder and the burner software. If your recorder works at lower recording speeds, the recordable media you have may not be certified for the higher speed, or it may just not work at the higher speed in your recorder. Brand new certified recording media often turns out to have physical flaws, which kind of defeats the point of it being "certified." Visually inspect the discs you are using and try recording at a higher speed with another brand. Successful recording at lower speed may also indicate a performance problem with the hard drive, the recorder or the operating system resources.

Does your recording software generate errors with cryptic code numbers? Recording software goes through frequent updates and requires high level access to the PC's resources. Previously installed recorder programs or even previous versions of the same software can cause errors in the management of the recording session. Check the software maker's website for a specific uninstall and clean-up utility before reinstalling the latest version.

Does the disc record properly, read or play fine in the drive you recorded it in, but fail to play in other computer drives or in consumer devices, such as stereos, DVD and Blu-ray players? The rewriteable media often fails completely in read-only drives, like standard CD ROM drives or DVD set-top boxes. Check with the manufacturer of the target device (the device you want to read the recorded disc in) to make sure you are using a compatible media and format. There are a sickening number of official formats and variations for recordable CDs and DVDs and many of them aren't supported by commercial playback devices,

and never will be. The rule of thumb for recording data discs that will be readable in the majority of "compatible" drives is to use the write-only media.

If you can read the disc in a drive other than the recorder but you get playback errors with movies, there's a good chance that a copy-protection scheme integrated into the recorder software is preventing you from making a clean copy. However, if the disc works fine in other drives, it's unclear at this point what the recording problem is.

Does the recording process continue to completion but the disc is unwritten? On most recordable media, you can easily tell whether or not the laser has written to the disc just by looking at the writeable surface of the disc and noting the circular tracks with lower reflectivity, where the laser has burned data. Compare with an unwritten disc if you aren't sure. Assuming you aren't running the burner software in "test" mode, which does everything but turn up the laser power to burn the disc, it means a problem with the laser. Either the lens is dirty (try a cleaning disc or disassembling the drive to clean by hand) or the laser is failing.

Is your hardware HDCP (High-bandwidth Digital Copy Protection) compliant? The HDCP standard is an anti-piracy measure developed by Intel which is supposed to prevent playing of hacked movies and creation of illegal copies. It primarily impacts high-definition media, and the hardware that must be certified includes video cards, set-top boxes, and recorders. If you are having trouble with recording only certain professional content, even if you are making a legitimate back-up, check whether the source is encrypted for HDCP.

Blu-ray recorders have extended the capacity of standard DVDs by a factor of five, from 4.7 GB for a single sided single layered DVD, to 25 GB for a single sided single layer Blu-ray disc, or 128 GB for a quadruple layer disc. But with all that capacity comes the requirement for computer hardware fast enough to read and process the stream of data. PC owners have long been used to being able to buy any peripherals sold in the store and assume that they will work with their systems as long as the operating system is up to date. Blu-ray drives require a fairly high performance CPU, and plenty of RAM and hard drive space. They also require a video card with 256 MB RAM, just for playing back high resolution movies. While PCs built and sold in the last few years will meet the requirements, an older low-cost consumer or business PC might not.

For high quality copying of music or video, digital extraction is the only way to go. Digital Audio Extraction (DAE) has long been available on most optical PC drives. On older DVD and CD drives, you need a hard wired connection between the DAE out from the drive and the sound card or motherboard. On newer DVD or Blu-ray drives, the DAE function should work over the SATA data cable, but check your drive to be sure.

There are too many available formats for audio and video to get into in a troubleshooting book, but the basic concept remains the same: garbage in, garbage out. You aren't going to get a copy that's better than the original source, so recording an early, low resolution MPEG file onto a Blu-ray disc isn't going to improve the playback, and the recording software may refuse to even work with the older formats. Most of the file formats are easily investigated by searching online, Wikipedia has some excellent write-ups. The only acronym you might trip over without recognizing is VCD (Video Compact Disc) which used the MPEG-1 CODEC to create video discs in older CD recorders. Note that many of the intermediate solutions for increasing capacity involved non-standard discs and recording practices, and these discs are rarely portable to a wide variety of playback devices.

Music CDs that you want to play in a stereo must be recorded on CDR, not CDRW, and the burner software must be set to record them in the CD-DA (Red Book) format. Writing a bunch of .wav files to a CD, even at the proper sampling frequency and in stereo, will not result in a CD that's playable in a stereo. It's the format that counts. You don't have to buy the more expensive CDR blanks labeled "CD Audio" or the like, these are only required for recording in dedicated (non PC connected) CDR devices. DVD players usually support multiple media types, but you need to check the documentation for the final word.

Finally, some manufactured discs are created with copy protection that can have unexpected results if you attempt to make copies. The copying process may go through without a hitch but leave you with a copy that doesn't play, or the software might report various errors. And some studio movie discs will not play in PCs if they employ protection that isn't incorporated into the latest version of the operating system media player. HDCP protection may allow extraction and recording but only at lower quality levels than the high-definition originals, so you may end up with CD quality sound rather than DVD quality sound, etc.

Modem Failure

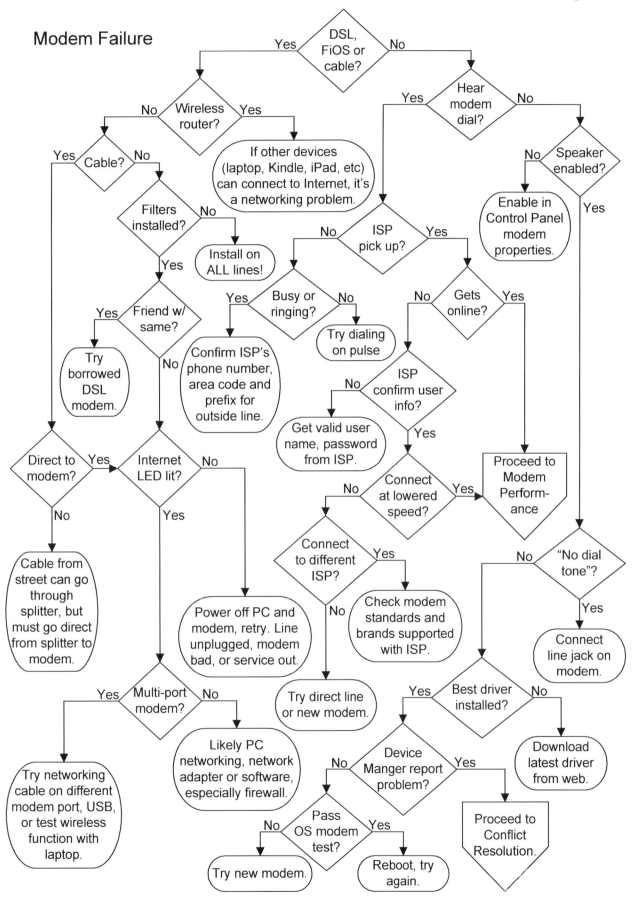

Modem Failure

Do you have a high speed Internet connection using the phone line for DSL (Digital Subscriber Line) and FiOS or through the cable TV network? The vast majority of high speed connections are accomplished through an external modem or modem/router, which provides for both the high speed connection to the Internet and supports connections to multiple PCs. Many new modems include a wireless router to support laptops and PCs, but the cheaper modems supplied by the carrier may only support a wired network or USB connection.

Can you hear your modem actually dial the phone? You should hear a dial tone when the modem first acquires the line, followed by tone or pulse dialing, depending which you've selected in software, tone being the default. Hearing what the modem is actually doing on the phone line is critical for troubleshooting.

Desktop PCs with discrete modems (a modem on an add-in adapter) have their own piezoelectric speaker on the circuit board, while "soft" modems integrated on the motherboard may use the PC speakers for sound. Many people (and computer vendors) turn down the volume for modems in software, which you can find on the "Properties" tab of the modems in Windows Control Panel. You should also make sure the volume controls in Windows are turned up and the speakers are turned on.

Does the ISP answer? You should be able to hear the ISP's modem pick up and whistle and hiss back at your modem through the speaker. If not, make sure you are dialing the right phone number and that the ISP isn't temporarily down. Just dial the number from a regular phone handset and the ISP modem should pick up and whistle at you.

Make sure you have the area code and any prefix for an outside line correct, especially if you are dialing from a business. Dial-up lines in a business must have a clean path through a business phone system (PBX - Private Branch eXchange), just like fax lines. If the phone is always busy, call the ISP's tech support or try one of the other phone numbers they provide. It could simply be that they don't have enough modems available for the traffic in your area at certain times of day.

If you hear the modem dial but the dial tone remains until an operator recording picks up and tells you that your phone is off hook, you're trying to use "tone" dialing on a "pulse" system. This is easily changed in the "Dialing Properties" of the basic modem page in Control Panel.

Do you get an error stating that the ISP can't negotiate a connection, protocol, anything along those lines? This counts as a "Yes" to "Gets Online?" Unfortunately, this error is too generic to help much with troubleshooting. Even messages telling you to check your password can be caused by just about anything. Try redialing several times without changing anything to make sure you aren't just encountering an overloaded modem pool. Proceed to Modem Performance troubleshooting.

Illustrated modem replacement:

www.fonerbooks.com /r_modem.htm

Call your ISP on the phone to confirm your login information if it's the first time you're dialing in. Re-enter your password, remembering that caps usually count, and make sure you aren't hitting Caps Lock instead of Shift to type a capital letter. If the error crops up at random, it's usually due to the weather and the time of day, as both play a major role in the circuit conditions of the telco infrastructure. Stormy or damp weather can badly degrade the lines of older telephone networks. The time of day is also important, with the beginning of the business day and a period in the mid-afternoon usually being the worst times. I've actually run non-Internet modem applications on dedicated lines that showed a huge increase of line noise during these periods, whatever your telco tells you.

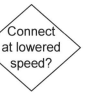

Will your modem connect at a lower speed? You can change the maximum speed the modem will try to connect at in Control Panel, but I've noted that the settings don't always take effect, even after rebooting. You can search on the Internet for the modem control string to force your modem to V.34 compatibility, then insert it in the Advanced Settings for the modem which can be accessed through the Modem Properties in Control Panel or Device Manager. If you succeed in connecting at a lower speed, try going through the Modem Performance diagnostics.

Can you connect to a different ISP? The best test for eliminating modem failure is to see if it will connect to a different service. If you can connect to a friend's ISP, it's a definite proof that the modem isn't bad. It doesn't mean that the ISP you can't connect to is at fault, it could be a question of matching modem standards. By the same token, if you can't connect to another ISP, it doesn't prove your modem is faulty, it could still be a problem with line conditions.

If the software reports "No Dial Tone" make sure you have the patch cord from the modem to the wall jack plugged into the "line" jack of the modem. The "phone" jack on the modem is for plugging in a regular telephone to use when you aren't online. If the wall jack is live, try changing the telephone patch cord running from the "line" jack on the modem to the jack on the wall. Check the phone jack at the wall with a telephone handset. If it doesn't work you need to repair the in-wall wiring or try a different jack.

Have you installed the most recent driver you can find on the modem manufacturer's web site? If your modem is integrated on the motherboard, it would be an update to your motherboard driver. Even if your modem is brand-new, hardware often ships with obsolete drivers, either because it's been sitting on the shelf somewhere for a year, or because a recent operating system release has overtaken it and a better driver is available.

Does the operating system report the modem as present and operating? This information appears in Device Manager in Windows. If not, reinstall the driver for the modem. If an IRQ conflict is reported in Device Manager, resolve it by either changing IRQ in software (with a plug-n-play modem) or changing the IRQ jumper on the modem for an old card. If you absolutely can't get around it, you may have an extremely unfriendly sound card or other adapter on the bus which is hogging the IRQ that the modem is capable of dealing with. Note that a modem can share an IRQ with legacy serial ports in some cases, though it can't be used when a device is actually attached to that port. If you can't resolve the Device Manager problem, either you have a hardware conflict, or the modem is bad. Proceed to the Conflict Resolution chart.

Does the operating system or dialing software report the port is "in use" when you try to dial? In Windows Control Panel > Modems, go to "Diagnostics," select your modem, and click on "More Info" or "Troubleshoot". Try shutting down and rebooting. The "port in use" error is due to another active software application claiming the port the modem is set on. You could get this error if you're already using the modem but don't realize it for some reason, but it's more likely that you've

recently installed software for synchronizing a legacy mobile device or camera that's colliding with the modem driver.

Is your modem a combination of a DSL, FiOS or cable modem with a wireless router? If other wireless devices can't connect to the Internet through the modem/router, continue with modem diagnostics from cable and DSL modems. If other devices (laptop, Kindle, iPad) do connect using the modem, the PC has a networking problem rather than a modem failure, and you should see the Network Hardware Diagnostics flowchart.

Do you have a cable modem? One of the DSL troubleshooting steps we skip is simply swapping your modem with that of a friend or neighbor who has the same model. While swapping might work in some cases, cable companies are far more finicky about installed hardware than phone companies due to their fear of people pirating cable signals, so it's not a useful test.

Is the cable from the street direct to the modem? Cable modems can't deal with too much signal degradation, and every junction and splitter between where the cable enters the house and the modem is a potential problem. The modem should be first in line, with only a single splitter that divides the incoming cable between the modem and the cable box at the TV. The splitter should be rated for the frequency of your cable system, so an old splitter you had around the house may not be sufficient. If the cable company has trouble reading the MAC address of your modem remotely during initial setup, it's a good sign that the signal is weak. Make sure the splitter isn't after the cable box, simply dividing the TV signal with the modem.

DSL and some FiOS modems are shipped from the Internet provider with a number of filters that you must install on every other phone connection on the circuit that's in use. Not installing the filters leads to two problems. First, you'll hear constant static on the regular phones when you try to talk. Second, some digital phone devices, such as answering machines or faxes, may also interfere with the DSL modem's ability to negotiate an Internet connection unless the filters are installed. Consult the instructions that come with the filters if you aren't sure where to use them. If you are setting up a DSL modem for the first time and can't get an Internet connection (assuming the phone company assures you it's live), you can also try unplugging any other phone devices in the house to make sure they aren't causing a problem.

One easy way to test if your DSL modem has failed on most systems is to borrow the identical working DSL modem from a friend or neighbor using the same system. Likewise, if your friends are brave, you can try installing your DSL modem on their line and seeing if it works, which eliminates the possibility that the modem is good and your incoming phone line has problems.

High speed modems, whether DSL, FiOS or cable, come equipped with a number of status LEDs that report on the condition of the modem. The LED we are interested in here is the one that reports on the status of the Internet connection to the modem. When the modem is powered on, this is the last LED to display a steady state status. Most modems also feature an LED that simply reports whether or not the modem sees a live connection to the cable company or to the phone company. When the Internet LED is off or red, make sure the cable, DSL or FiOS line is connected, turn off the modem and the PC and try restarting just the modem, giving it a few minutes to negotiate the connection. The problem might be that service in your area is out, but check the obvious before calling the provider.

If your modem only supports a single networking connection and USB, but you can't get online with your PC, try changing to the other connection and reinstalling the software supplied by the service provider. Replace the networking or USB cable with a known good cable. If you have a true modem/router, try connecting the networking cable from your PC to a different port, even if the status LED indicated the other port connection was good. If the router supports wireless, borrow a laptop and see if you can get online, and then turn off wireless and connect the laptop directly to eliminate the possibility that you have a failed network adapter or bad USB port in the PC.

If the hardware all tests good through the laptop or through your taking it to a friend's to test, and your PC network adapter or USB port are also working, the problem is software settings. Uninstall the software from the Internet provider and then try reinstalling, making sure you follow their instructions to the letter about the sequence of steps. Make sure your virus suite and firewall software aren't blocking Internet access and contact the tech support for your Internet provider who can walk you through all of the settings in Windows.

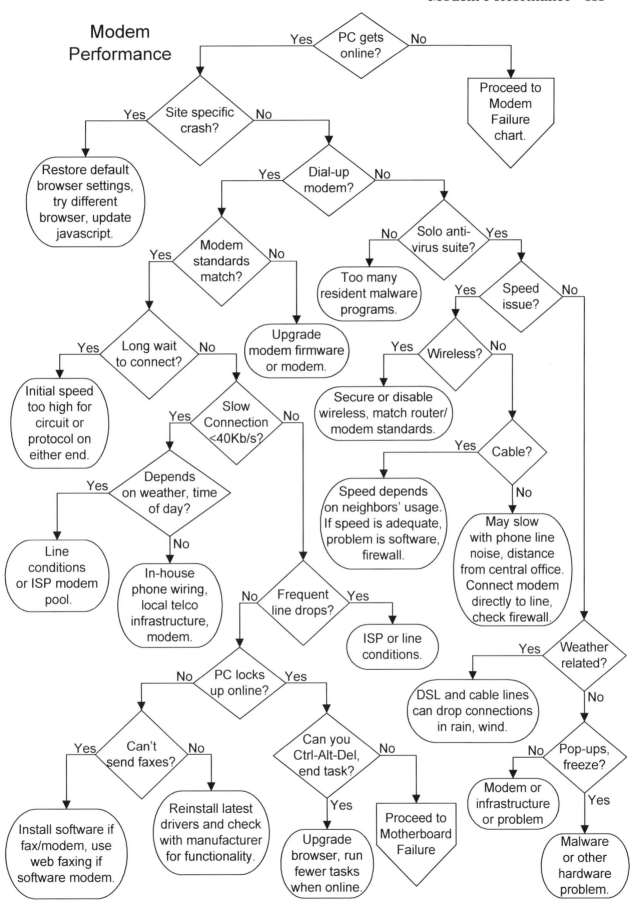

Modem
Performance

Yes — PC gets online? — No

Proceed to Modem Failure chart.

Yes — Site specific crash? — No

Restore default browser settings, try different browser, update javascript.

Yes — Dial-up modem? — No

No — Solo anti-virus suite? — Yes

Too many resident malware programs.

Yes — Modem standards match? — No

Upgrade modem firmware or modem.

Yes — Speed issue? — No

Yes — Long wait to connect? — No

Initial speed too high for circuit or protocol on either end.

Yes — Wireless? — No

Secure or disable wireless, match router/modem standards.

Slow Connection <40Kb/s? — No

Speed depends on neighbors' usage. If speed is adequate, problem is software, firewall.

Yes — Cable? — No

Yes — Depends on weather, time of day? — No

Line conditions or ISP modem pool.

In-house phone wiring, local telco infrastructure, modem.

May slow with phone line noise, distance from central office. Connect modem directly to line, check firewall.

No — Frequent line drops? — Yes

ISP or line conditions.

Yes — Weather related? — No

DSL and cable lines can drop connections in rain, wind.

No — PC locks up online? — Yes

Yes — Can't send faxes? — No

Can you Ctrl-Alt-Del, end task? — No

No — Pop-ups, freeze? — Yes

Install software if fax/modem, use web faxing if software modem.

Reinstall latest drivers and check with manufacturer for functionality.

Upgrade browser, run fewer tasks when online.

Proceed to Motherboard Failure

Modem or infrastructure or problem

Malware or other hardware problem.

Modem Performance

Can you access the Internet through your PC and modem combination? We're talking about getting online, being able to run an Internet search or access your e-mail. If not, see the modem failure flowchart.

Does your browser routinely lock-up or even crash the PC when you visit a particular website? Try restoring the advanced settings in your browser to the defaults if you've made any changes, and see whether the problem is browser specific by downloading another free browser. The main reason for lock-ups or pauses so long that they make you believe the browser is frozen is the video based advertising that eats bandwidth and challenges lower performance PCs to run the scripts. There's always the possibility of a hacked website with malware as well.

Old fashioned dial-up modems actually have far more performance related problems than newer high speed modems connected to the phone company by DSL or to the cable provider via a cable modem. The one thing they all have in common is that if your PC has been taken over by malware, it will run slow no matter how you connect.

Does your modem standard match one of the modem standards supported by the ISP? The most recent standard for 56K dial-up modems is V.92, though some of ISPs may still use V.90. The two previous 56K standards supported by some rural ISPs are k56Flex and X2. The previous 33K standards, V.32 and V.34 are probably more universally supported than the early 56K standards. Many of the 33K pre-V.90 modems can actually be upgraded to V.90 through a flash upgrade of the adapter BIOS, obtained through the manufacturer.

Almost all modems sold in the last fifteen years will support V.90 or V.92, but some ISP's have yet to implement it and are still running one of the original 56K standards, k56Flex or X2. Often times, local ISPs don't really know what they are doing and will blame any problems on your modem, until you buy one that happens to match their network. If your ISP claims to support all of these but "suggests" you try V.90, I'd take that to mean that their support is conditional, and you're better off getting a V.90 or V.92 modem if you want to connect to them with any success. Before you replace a modem, you should really try it with another ISP. If it works fine with them, you can make an informed decision as to whether you want to play musical modems until you get one that your current ISP is compatible with, or jump ship.

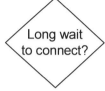

Does it take your modem up to a half a minute or longer to obtain a connection after the answering modem picks up? There are several possibilities, but the most likely is that your modem is capable of a much higher connection speed than the circuit, for various reasons, can support. The endless negotiation between your modem and the ISP modem can be a result of slowly ratcheting down the speed on both ends until a satisfactory error rate is reached. This could be due to a failing modem, but it's more often infrastructure or line conditions that limit connection speed.

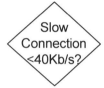

Is your connection speed always much lower than the modem rating? Most people have 56K modems that should get connections ranging from 40K to 53K in ideal conditions. It could be that your modem speed is actually set too low in software, or that you are using some error checking or compression algorithm that isn't ideal for the circuit. Make a note of all of your current settings before you start making changes, and note that in some cases, you'll have to reboot before they take effect. Make sure you check the Extra Settings field in the modem connection Advanced Properties menu. It could also be that your phone wiring simply isn't going to support a higher speed, that you are too far from the central office, or they just haven't upgraded their infrastructure to support digital signaling, in which case you'll never get a connection over 33K. Your ISP may not really support higher speeds, or they may have a mix of modem banks such that your connection speed appears to be random.

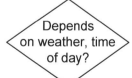

If your connection speed depends on the weather or the time of day, it's probably due to line conditions. The worst times to dial into the web are usually at the start of the business day and when school lets out. This is due to the noise on the copper phone lines generated by the heavy use at these times. The weather effect depends on the quality of your telephone company infrastructure. I have firsthand experience with poor local infrastructure murdering connection speed. My old notebook computer rarely got connections over 33K and suffered frequent line-drops when dialing into a local ISP. When I took the notebook on a trip to Florida, 1100 miles away, and dialed into the same ISP phone number by long distance, I got

stable 52K connections every time. The area of Florida I was
visiting had new phone infrastructure using lots of fiber optics,
as opposed to the 80 year old copper in my New England town!

Do you suffer from frequent disconnects? The first thing to
check if you have line drops is whether you have call waiting and
a modem/ISP that doesn't support call waiting. If you don't have
call waiting, line drops are usually a result of the ISP being over
burdened, or are caused by really bad line conditions. The ISP
will rarely admit that their system is dropping lines, so it's a
tough one to diagnose with 100% certainty. There's nothing you
can do about the telco infrastructure, but you can get the
cleanest connection possible in your house by reducing the
number of connections between your PC and the incoming
phone line. You can also try running your modem at a lower
speed. In extreme cases, you can try replacing your modem, but
I'd probably try a new ISP first. You may determine that the
problem is with the infrastructure of the telephone company or
some other external factors, such as the wiring in your part of
town being routed alongside an incredibly noisy electrical
transformer, etc. There's nothing you can do about the weather,
but you can work around the time of day problem by identifying
the good times to call in and sticking with them.

Does the whole computer sometimes lock up when you're
online, forcing you to shut down and reboot? If it always
happens at the same web site, it's probably an incompatibility
with the web browser version and software plug-ins. You may
need to enable Java Script or download and install a browser
upgrade to access certain sites. The important thing to
understand is if the lock-up only occurs on certain sites, it's not
a modem issue.

If you can get a live task list with ctrl-alt-del, shut down the
browser and continue, it's probably a software conflict or an
incompatible web application. Browsers sometimes lock up if
you try to access your favorites list before the browser has
finished loading. You could also be suffering lock-ups due to
lack of RAM or CPU overheating problems, so start again at the
Motherboard, CPU and RAM Failure diagnostics.

Do you want to send or receive faxes but you can't figure out
how? The first thing to check is whether or not you have a
fax/modem. If it wasn't sold as a fax/modem and the driver
doesn't identify it as a fax modem, it's not a fax and you can't
directly use it to send and receive faxes. You can still use a web

based fax service. If you do have a fax/modem and can't fax, it's just a question of installing (or finding) the proper software, which should have come on CD with the fax/modem.

Do you have an anti-virus suite installed that handles the firewall, virus scanning, malware, a link scanner, e-mail scanning and an anti-root kit? If so, you shouldn't have any other memory resident virus or malware software running or the programs will end up duplicating each other's activity, scanning the same potential threats multiple times and eating both memory and CPU cycles. If you don't have an all-in-one suite, make sure that the individual components you've installed don't overlap in functionality for the same reason given above.

Does it seem like your high speed connection isn't that fast? Malware and viruses can kill your performance, but so can aggressive firewall settings, which is why most firewall software includes a lower security setting for when you are running online games which require maximum interactivity and performance. In order to test your physical connection speed before you complain to your Internet provider, check their website for a speed testing tool, or try a third party speed checker.

Does your modem/router support a wireless connection? If it does, have you established a secure password for accessing the Internet? If you live in an urban area and you haven't secured your modem, it's almost a given that neighbors will be borrowing some of your bandwidth with their laptops, often unintentionally because they simply connect to the network that works. If there's a wireless LED on your modem/router and it's going nuts when you aren't using a laptop yourself, create a wireless password or disable the wireless function.

If you're running the PC over wireless rather than wiring directly to the router with a network cable, make sure the router and the PC both support the same wireless standard or one will be slowing down for the other. Wireless routers and receivers are usually backwards compatible, so a B/G/N suffix means it supports all three of those generations.

Are you running a cable modem? Unlike DSL modems which are directly connected to the phone company central office by your phone line, cable modems are pooled together in such a way that they share the available bandwidth in the neighborhood. If your speed varies widely throughout the day, there's nothing wrong with your connection, it's just a question of usage patterns. If you have some neighbors who spend all their waking hours downloading movies from the Internet, you just aren't going to see the maximum cable performance. As with all modems, it's also a good idea to make your cable connection as clean as possible, eliminating extra switches and splitters between the modem and the incoming line.

DSL modems must be within a few miles of the phone switching office to work, and as you get near the limits, the performance may drop off due to higher error rates. You might also see performance degradation with weather conditions or during high phone use periods during the business day, something FiOS avoids. Make sure that you are using filters on all phone extensions with devices (phones, answering machines, etc) connected. If benchmarking software shows you aren't getting the speed you are paying for, your only choice may be cable.

Do you get frequent disconnects or lock-ups during inclement weather? Outside of the most modern urban areas with buried services and high-rise buildings, both cable and DSL are delivered to the home through lines strung on phone poles. The mechanical stress relief on those lines can be taxed in windy conditions, and can be damaged by falling branches and vehicles colliding with poles. Sunlight and aging can also crack the insulation on lines allowing in moisture during rain and snow.

Weather related performance hits are due to the condition of the infrastructure outside of your house, so you'll have to be very specific about what is happening when you call the cable or phone company for service, which should be free since they own the outside infrastructure. If you don't specify that the performance degradation comes with the rain or the storm, they may just test the connection at the time you call-in, and of course, it will test out fine on a sunny day with no wind.

Cable, DSL and FiOS connected PCs will all see a huge knock on performance if they have been taken over by malware. If you aren't running a virus protection suite including anti-virus, anti-adware and a firewall, you should install one. If your PC behaves strangely, if your home page has changed to some generic looking directory site you've never heard of or if you get endless pop-ups trying to sell you things, your PC has been infected or hijacked by malware. However, if your PC frequently freezes up or generates cryptic messages about memory errors, it's more likely that you have a hardware problem, and should refer to the Motherboard, CPU and RAM Performance flowchart first.

If your Internet connection works fast when it's working, but frequently disconnects or glitches, it's likely a modem problem or a problem with the service provider. Don't be afraid to call tech support to complain, but first start a log of when and in what circumstances the problems occur. Not only will that help convince the service provider that you're serious, it may help you diagnose the problem before you have to spend an hour on the phone trying to get through to a human being. Cable modem wiring within the house tends to be simpler than DSL wiring, since you have a limited number of cable devices. If you are using multiple telephone line splitters in the connection to your DSL modem, it could be something as silly as a poor connection in one of them that gets shaken up when you use a particular phone extension. Always connect your DSL modem directly into a telephone wall jack.

Sound Failure

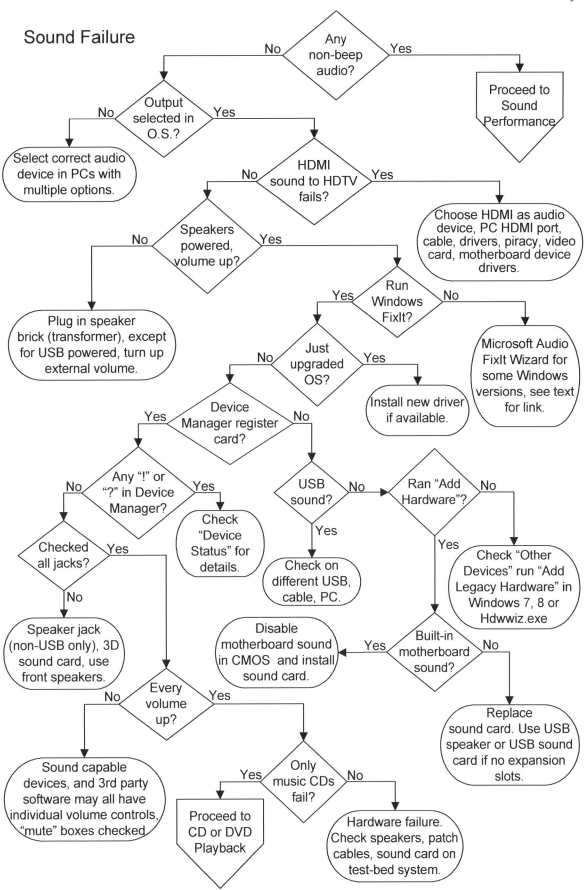

Sound Failure

Do you get any audio out of the PC other than beeps on power-up? The beeps you hear on power-up are not part of the PC's sound system, they are generated by a tiny piezoelectric speaker on the motherboard that is included strictly for diagnostic codes. If you are getting any other audio from the playback device you have selected (speakers, HDTV, headset), that sound hardware hasn't failed, so you can proceed to the sound performance flowchart.

Windows will normally only process sound through one audio device at a time, and this will be whatever default audio device is chosen, unless the application does the switching for you. The audio playback device list is accessed different ways in different versions of Windows, but you can always find it through Control Panel under the generic Sounds and Audio Devices. There may be a number of different brand name audio controls on your Windows Desktop or in Control Panel by the time you're finished installing driver software for all of your hardware. This is what makes software audio troubleshooting so confusing, but at this point, you need the screen that allows you to choose the default device for both playback and recording.

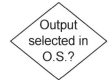

Are you unable to play audio through an HDTV connected by an HDMI cable to the graphics adapter or motherboard? As long as you are using the proper HDMI cable and are plugged into PC HDMI port on the TV (assuming it has one) the problem is likely with software. Make sure that you have chosen the HDMI sound device for your output in Windows and that you have the latest drivers installed for your video card and motherboard, whichever hosts the HDMI device. And remember that there is a hardware level anti-piracy component, HDCP (High-bandwidth Digital Content Protection) to playing high definition movies with DVD quality sound, which may prevent non HDCP certified hardware from playing movie audio.

Are the speakers plugged in to a power source? If there is an external volume control on speakers, it will serve as an on/off as well. USB speakers can draw DC power from the USB port, but most PC speakers include a power cord or transformer. Really ancient amplified speakers may be powered by batteries rather than a transformer, so if your speakers don't have a power cord, double check that they don't have a hatch for batteries. Note also that some of the oldest sound cards had a manual volume dial,

so if you see one, adjust it to somewhere in the middle of the range, not all the way to one extreme or the other.

For Windows PCs, have you run the Microsoft FixIt wizard for audio problems? While it doesn't work for every version of Windows and could be discontinued at any time, it's worth trying to find it at:

http://support.microsoft.com/mats/audioplayback

The FixIt wizard checks many of the issues detailed in the following troubleshooting chart steps, including conflicting software settings that can be very time consuming to find and check yourself.

Have you recently upgraded the operating system and are now trying to play a particular movie, CD or game for the first time since? The old device driver might not work with the new operating system or it might give the software only partial access to the hardware's capabilities, but in all cases, you should upgrade the drivers. If you have an add-in sound card, this means downloading a driver from the sound card maker. If you have HDMI sound through your add-in video adapter, download a new driver from the video adapter manufacturer website. If the audio is integrated on the motherboard, you'll need new drivers from either the motherboard manufacturer, the PC manufacturer (if it's a brand name), or the audio chipset maker (RealTek, VIA, etc), whichever is actually providing the updates.

Does Device Manager register the sound card or integrated motherboard audio and report that the device is working properly? Even if you don't have the proper driver, Device Manager will probably identify the audio hardware as a sound controller. Before you start stripping down the system or chase off to conflict resolution, make sure sound isn't disabled in CMOS or the add-in adapter is seated in the motherboard slot.

If Device Manager reports a resource conflict between any of the audio devices and another device, look through all of your device reports and figure out where the conflict is. It may be resolvable by changing the settings in Device Manager, or it may take aggressive reshuffling of adapters. If you get a "!", "?" or "i" on the sound controller in Device Manager, proceed to Conflict Resolution for older legacy hardware.

Check your documentation or the symbols on the sound card to make sure you actually have the speakers plugged into the proper jack. Modern sound cards and motherboards with 3-D sound (5.1, 6.1 and 7.1 3-D) have jacks for up to eight speakers. Try testing through the front speaker jacks only. Check that your audio patch cables are all plugged firmly into the proper jacks and that the cables aren't damaged. If you have USB speakers, they don't jack directly into the sound card.

Software volume controls are the #1 nuisance problem with sound, and a real pain to figure out if multiple people use the system. Aside from the primary volume control often found in your system tray, there are various other mixer panels and volume adjustments that get installed with the driver(s) and are offered in various applications. All of these can cause a complete absence of sound if the "mute" box is checked. There's no magic method for finding the mixer panel or any additional volume controls in a typical system, though the Windows FixIt wizard mentioned on the previous page can help.

Does your sound system work properly with everything except music CDs? If so, proceed to CD and DVD Playback diagnostics. Otherwise, unless you missed a software setting, the problem is either the external hardware or the sound card output stage being blown. A good test is to try the speakers and cables on another system, or another device with a speaker jack, like a portable radio. Make sure you first turn the speaker volume control all the way down in case the output is already amplified. If your speakers and cables don't work anywhere, try swapping the cables to find out which is faulty. If the speakers and cables are good, either the sound card is blown or you didn't look hard enough for a hidden mute in software.

If you are using USB speakers or a full USB sound card, try connecting them to a different USB port. USB ports often break inside the PC when the cords are jerked or tripped over. If you can't get the USB sound device to function on the PC, test it on any other PC or laptop. If it works on another computer, you know that the problem is either that all of your USB ports have failed (which would usually mean the USB controller on the motherboard popped), that the driver software is incompatible, or that you didn't find a "mute" in the OS. Note also that amplified USB speakers may require more current that an older version USB port supplies, and may not operate properly through an unpowered USB hub.

Have you run the "Add New Hardware" wizard to try to encourage Device Manage to find the sound hardware? Device Manager will normally spot new hardware the first time Windows boots with it, but sometimes a manual search is required. In Windows 7 and Windows 8, the "Add New Hardware" wizard has been replaced by the "Add Legacy Hardware," which can also be accessed by running Hdwwiz.exe. If your sound hardware isn't found, check the "Other Devices" category to see if Windows is locating the hardware but not recognizing its purpose, which may be corrected if you can get the driver installed.

If your only audio support is built into the motherboard, make sure it's enabled in CMOS Setup. If you are using a sound card, make sure any motherboard audio is disabled in CMOS Setup. The easiest way to replace a motherboard integrated sound card is to pick up USB speakers (the sound card is built into the speakers) or a full USB sound hub. The only potential problem with these is if you have an older CD or DVD drive that doesn't support DAE (Digital Audio Extraction) through the motherboard interface. Without DAE through the motherboard controller, USB sound devices won't be able to play music CDs.

Illustrated sound card replacement

www.fonerbooks.com
/r_sound.htm

If you can't get the operating system to recognize an installed sound card, which is sure to be plug-and-play, shut down and unplug, remove all the other adapters except the video card from the system, reboot and let the BIOS and operating system adjust. Then shut down and unplug again, add the sound card, and see if you can get it going. If this works, you might still have problems when you add the other adapters back in, but if you do it one at a time, at least you'll find out for sure where the conflict lies.

Sound Performance

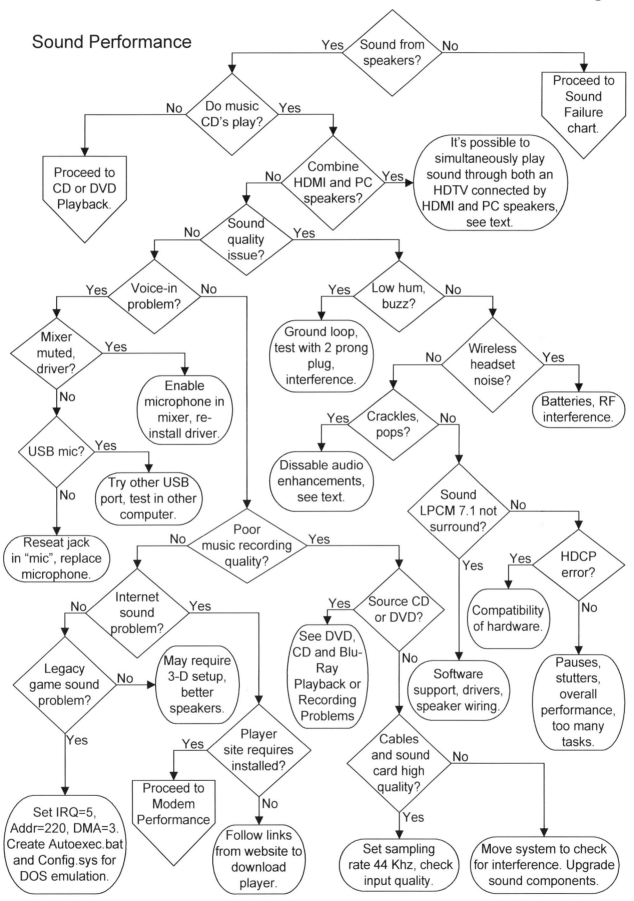

Sound from speakers?
— Yes → Do music CD's play?
— No → Proceed to Sound Failure chart.

Do music CD's play?
— No → Proceed to CD or DVD Playback.
— Yes → Combine HDMI and PC speakers?

Combine HDMI and PC speakers?
— No → Sound quality issue?
— Yes → It's possible to simultaneously play sound through both an HDTV connected by HDMI and PC speakers, see text.

Sound quality issue?
— No → Voice-in problem?
— Yes → Low hum, buzz?

Voice-in problem?
— Yes → Mixer muted, driver?
— No → Poor music recording quality?

Mixer muted, driver?
— Yes → Enable microphone in mixer, re-install driver.
— No → USB mic?

USB mic?
— Yes → Try other USB port, test in other computer.
— No → Reseat jack in "mic", replace microphone.

Low hum, buzz?
— Yes → Ground loop, test with 2 prong plug, interference.
— No → Wireless headset noise?

Wireless headset noise?
— No → Crackles, pops?
— Yes → Batteries, RF interference.

Crackles, pops?
— Yes → Dissable audio enhancements, see text.
— No → Sound LPCM 7.1 not surround?

Sound LPCM 7.1 not surround?
— Yes → Compatibility of hardware.
— No → HDCP error?

HDCP error?
— Yes → Software support, drivers, speaker wiring.
— No → Pauses, stutters, overall performance, too many tasks.

Poor music recording quality?
— No → Internet sound problem?
— Yes → Source CD or DVD?

Internet sound problem?
— No → Legacy game sound problem?
— Yes → May require 3-D setup, better speakers.

Legacy game sound problem?
— No → May require 3-D setup, better speakers.
— Yes → Set IRQ=5, Addr=220, DMA=3. Create Autoexec.bat and Config.sys for DOS emulation.

Player site requires installed?
— Yes → Proceed to Modem Performance
— No → Follow links from website to download player.

Source CD or DVD?
— Yes → See DVD, CD and Blu-Ray Playback or Recording Problems
— No → Cables and sound card high quality?

Cables and sound card high quality?
— Yes → Set sampling rate 44 Khz, check input quality.
— No → Move system to check for interference. Upgrade sound components.

Sound Performance

Do you get any sound out of the speakers when the computer boots? If not, unless you've intentionally turned off the operating system sounds, proceed to Sound Failure diagnostics.

Can you hear a music CD through the speakers when the operating system shows that one is being played? Note, if you can't even get the Media Player software to report that it's playing the CD, you either have a Media Player or drive problem rather than an audio problem. Unless you have USB speakers, proceed to the CD or DVD Performance chart. If you do have USB speakers, your CD player and your motherboard ATA controller must support Digital Audio Extraction (DAE) for the digital stream to be fed to the speakers. The DAE output on older CD or DVD drives without analog audio must be hooked to the proper port on the sound card or motherboard as well.

Are you trying to set your PC up to play HDMI sound to the TV while still using the PC's speaker system? Windows wants you to select a default audio output device, which for this application should be the PC sound card which powers the PC speakers. If you are running one of the new Windows versions, you should be able to check off "show disabled devices" on the Recording tab, and enable the mixing device that appears – look for an updated driver if the option doesn't appear. Set it as the default device (right click), choose "Properties" for the device and under the "Listen" tab, click "Listen to this device" and add HDMI to the "Playback through this device" list. Just be aware that if it works for you, you'll have to go back and change the default recording device any time you actually want to record audio.

Is the problem with the quality of the audio playback? The diagnostics split here between issues relating to poor quality audio and issues involving aspects of the sound system not working. The latter case includes instances where music and movies play fine, but recorded sound is poor, the mic doesn't work, certain Internet applications don't play sound properly, or legacy games fail to play audio.

Is your problem with voice recording, Skype or speech recognition? Check that you have the mic in the proper port. If you are doing speech recognition, you should purchase a quality noise cancellation mic and go through the calibration and testing procedures your software will include. Make sure that the audio driver for the mic is set to the maximum quality. Skype setup does a good job testing your microphone and reporting on the quality. If you still have a mic quality problem, the cheapest and easiest solution is to pick up a USB mic, or you can buy a USB sound card with a mic jack. Otherwise, you may need to replace your sound card, or disable motherboard audio and install a sound card.

Make sure that the microphone isn't muted in the software mixer panel. Check Device Manager for any problems, and if there are any warnings ("!", "?", "i") next to the sound card, reinstall the driver. If reinstalling the driver doesn't clear up the warning, proceed to Conflict Resolution for legacy PCs. If the mute box is unchecked and there isn't a driver problem, continue to "USB mic?"

First, try the mic on a different USB port. A USB microphone also serves as a sound card, since its communication with the PC is strictly digital. That means that the PC's sound card isn't involved at all with the troubleshooting, and you can easily test whether or not the USB mic is working properly by trying it on any other PC or laptop. If the USB mic is good but it doesn't work properly on your PC, there's a problem with your USB ports, the overall performance of the PC being too slow, or with the particular recording software you are using.

If you aren't using a USB mic, double check that the microphone jack is in the "mic" port, and if it still fails, try the microphone on another audio device and replace it if it's bad. If the microphone is good, it means that just that part of your sound card or motherboard sound has failed. Check the physical jack leads on the sound card or motherboard to make sure one of them hasn't broken from the solder. If you are otherwise happy with the way your sound card performs, add a USB mic to the PC rather than replacing the motherboard or add-in sound card.

Does the music you record sound poor when you play it back? Check your patch cables and jacks for loose connections. Some cables are extremely low quality, so if you plan to do a lot of audio work, start by getting a good set. Make sure that your mixer settings (the software mixer panel) aren't uneven, muting the channels you want, or simply running an unexpected mix. Try muting any inactive channels, like "line" if you are recording off of "mic" or muting "mic" if recording off "line" since unused inputs can introduce white noise. Don't neglect to check the quality of the audio source. If you're trying to record from a hissing tape or a scratchy recording, the sound card does not automatically filter out the unwanted noise. High end recording software does give you the option to clean up recordings, but usually after the recording process is complete.

The quality of any sound recorder is limited by the quality of the source. If you are recording from a CD or DVD, you should be using Digital Audio Extraction (DAE) to make a copy of the audio source files, not playing back through a sound card. Anti-piracy schemes accomplished in hardware may prevent you from recording high quality audio from some sources. See the DVD, CD and Blu-ray Playback flowchart.

First, check the sampling rate is set to 44 kHz (audio CD quality) or higher. Interference is always a possibility, especially if it takes the form of loud ticking. Try moving the system to another location if you're recording near any electrical motors or other possible sources of low frequency interference. True audiophiles spend hundreds of dollars (or more) on audio patch cables that could be worn as jewellery, given the rare metals the wiring is drawn from. They also spend hundreds of dollars on sound cards, and although these are marketed for their playback rather than recording quality, you may get what you pay for.

Is your problem related to playing Internet radio or other web based audio applications? If the quality stinks, it's probably your connection to the Internet, so see the Modem Performance flowchart. If you have a broadband (cable, DSL) connection and the quality still bad, check your download speed using a reputable speed testing site. It could also be that the Internet site is streaming low quality audio, that your PC is under-powered and you're running too many tasks at the same time, or the hard drive is near full and virtual memory is thrashing it.

Some Internet audio applications use a third party player, such as Real Audio. If you get no Internet sound at all, but all other audio applications work, your OS and the player software aren't getting along. All you can do is to try reinstalling the latest edition. There's usually a link to a site from which you can download a free copy of the player, though it can take a while and you may have to reboot when it's done.

There are a number of reasons the sound quality on your system may not match your experience on somebody else's machine. You may have previously played a game on a better system than yours, one that supported 3D sound with more or better

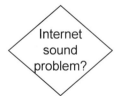

arranged speakers than you have. The sound card or motherboard audio in your system may be lower quality. The same for the speakers. You could also be picking up interference on the speaker wires, so try routing them away from the computer (and especially keep them away from the monitor).

Is the audio problem with an older game? Rather than try to differentiate between older and newer games, this question could be, "Does sound work properly with other games?" Ancient games may need obsolete sound card compatibility. The default settings of IRQ=5, Address=220, DMA=5 are usually required, since the game communicates directly with the sound card. You may be able to force your sound card to these settings, or, when supported by the driver, you might get by with emulating them under the sound card setup in Device Manager. There's also the possibility, if your game actually exits and runs in DOS mode, that you need to have the proper drivers installed in the DOS Startup files, config.sys and autoexec.bat.

Do you hear a low pitched buzz or hum coming through the speakers? The leading cause of speaker hum is ground loops, which can be tested by moving the power brick (AC transformer) for the amplified speakers to another circuit or eliminating the ground prong by putting a 3-prong to 2-prong converter in between the plug and the socket. If it eliminates the noise, you've found the problem, but we don't recommend operating permanently with the ground eliminated, it's there for safety. You can purchase an inline isolation transformer that will eliminate the noise, but do the test first to make sure that's the problem.

The other possibilities include poor speaker wires, faulty jacks, and interference. Try unplugging the speakers one at a time and see if that eliminates the issue. It's always possible that an amplified speaker is creating the noise on its own in the amplification stage. Also, check that the speaker wire routing doesn't take it close to a low frequency noise source, like a transformer for a laptop, which can add noise to the line.

If you're hearing noise on a wireless headset, it almost always comes down to one of two issues. First, the batteries are getting low and the voltage is dropping. It's the same as wireless phones in houses, when the battery starts to run down, they get noisy. Second, you have may have an interference issue. It could be something in the room, like a wireless phone or a noisy transformer, or it could be any nearby electrical emitter that runs intermittently. If you establish that the noise comes and goes, try taking off the headphones when the interference starts and listen for any appliances in the house or outdoor equipment running. If the headset noise goes away when the whole house air conditioner cycles off or the lawn tractor moves away from the window, you've found the problem.

Do you hear crackles and pops from the speakers? Loose jacks and cables can cause popping noises, but it's also possible that you have Audio Enhancements turned on in a newer Windows version and the hardware isn't up to it. On the "Playback" tab of "Sound" reached through Control Panel, click "Properties" followed by "Enhancements" and disable all enhancements. If this fixes the problem, there's a chance that a newer sound card driver will correct the issue. If you don't have the enhancements option, you should still try updating the sound card driver, as long as newer version is available.

Do you have all of the speakers set up for a 3-D or surround sound system but you never hear the monster creeping up behind you to cut your head off in your favorite game? Start with the obvious, like running the test software that comes with the audio driver (after all of your speakers are hooked up), so you can hear each speaker individually. If any of the speakers fail the test, try swapping speakers to determine if it's the speaker, the cable or the audio device. If all of the hardware is working, make sure you have the latest driver installed and check the game maker's website for the compatibility of the game with the hardware and standard you are running. If the sound works in all but one particular game, the only answer to be found will be through their support forum.

Do you get an HDCP (High-bandwidth Digital Content Protection) error on playback? HDCP requires certified hardware to play high definition movies and audio. If the HDMI output on your HDCP certified video card doesn't see an HDCP certified device on the other end of the cable, it won't allow the playback of DVD quality audio. You may get an error message or you may not notice the difference. These errors may be seen when you try to play studio content to high definition TV's using the wrong HDMI port or when you are missing a software CODEC (COder/DECoder) required for the particular DVD or Blu-ray disc.

For more general audio performance problems, like pauses in playback, or stutters, the issue is likely the media or the overall performance of the PC. If you are playing a disc, make sure that it is clean, try to play the disc in another PC, and it can't hurt to run a cleaning disc for the laser in the drive. Try playing the same disc right after you turn on the PC, to see if programs you are manually starting are killing performance and interrupting the playback. You can try booting in Safe Mode as well, or manually shutting down programs that are auto-started when your PC is turned on.

Network Hardware Diagnostics

Wired LAN?

No → PC see network?

Yes → Works unsecured?

No → Wireless enabled, router active, range, hidden network.

Yes → Password or protocol incorrect.

No → Works cabled direct?

Yes → MAC address, firewall?

Yes → Add MAC to approved table, modify firewall settings.

No → Check network or Internet is live at wireless router.

No → Default settings on router?

Yes → Loses signal, slow?

No → Restore default settings, if wired connection won't work, WiFi won't work.

No → Other WiFi devices work?

Yes → Try updating the driver for your WiFi adapter. For Internet related issues, see Modem Performance flowchart.

No → Router failing, bridge to network or Internet connection bad.

Yes → Same (B/G/N) 802.11

Yes → Interference, PC WiFi adapter bad, PC location out of range, router.

No → Upgrade all network hardware to latest standard.

Yes → Random problems?

No → New hub added to LAN?

No → Link light lit?

Yes → Copied network config?

No → Clone setup from good workstation.

Yes → Device Manager problem?

Yes → Update driver, replace card, see Conflict Resolution

No → Tried different port on hub?

No → Physical layer (cables, devices)

Yes → Check crossover (X) port wiring.

Yes → Wiggled cable?

No → Flex the cable at back of PC and watch link LED to test RJ-45 connector.

Within physical layer limits?

Yes → Tried different port on hub?

No → Add repeaters, re-route cables.

Yes → Fails on traffic, # of users?

Yes → Swap hub for switch, check server utilization.

No → Flaky off network also?

Yes → Proceed to Motherboard Performance.

No → Cable bypass to hub fix?

Yes → Bad patch or in-wall cabling.

No → New network card works?

No → Most likely software conflicts, setup or virus.

Yes → Throw out old adapter, $10 new.

If connection stable on new port, prior port is failing.

Network Hardware Diagnostics

Are you troubleshooting PCs on a wired LAN (Local Area Network) or a WiFi network? In previous versions of this book we assumed that PCs, as opposed to laptops, would generally be connected to corporate and home networks by Ethernet cables. But brand-name PC manufacturers have started including WiFi adapters in desktop PCs, and most homes with broadband probably have a wireless router for laptops, iPads and Kindles, so wireless networking of PCs is becoming common. Just keep in mind that going wireless will generally mean taking a big performance hit over the latest wired LAN technology.

Are you having random network connectivity problems, as opposed to never being able to access a server or the Internet, depending on the purpose of your LAN? If there are multiple users on the network, check to see if you are all experiencing the same problems at the same times, which would mean that your PC hardware isn't the problem, in which case you should answer "No" to the question. If your PC is the only one having random problems, run the latest malware scan and check the Windows CPU and memory performance monitor to make sure your overall system isn't bogging down before continuing.

Network adapters are universally included in the motherboard I/O core in new PCs, but there should still be at least one LED next to the port to show the status of the link to the hub. If the LED blinks when you wiggle the cord, either the RJ-45 connector is loose on the cable (highly likely) or the port in the I/O core has a broken lead. Some network ports, especially those on add-in adapters, may have a separate LED for link status and activity, otherwise they use the same LED for both, blinking it when the PC is communicating with the network.

Are the cable runs within the physical layer limits for the networking hardware? You can't count on using the maximum distance defined by the IEE 802.11 network standard, you have to use the lowest number given by any of the hardware components (hubs, routers, network adapters) on the LAN. And remember that all distances are actual cable lengths, not measurements from a blueprint. If you're using repeaters to boost the signal, there are limits there as well since the distances affect transmission times and can lead to time-out problems if the setup is finicky.

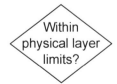

Did you add a new router or hub to the LAN? We all fall into the trap of assuming that new equipment will work when we take it out of the box, especially if the LEDs light up when it's plugged in. So if you've installed a new hub or router and the workstation you're having trouble with is wired through it, the first test is to move the workstation's patch cord to a port on another router to eliminate the port you were using on the new router as the issue. Just for the record, a network hub is a switching point within the network, while a router technically comes between networks. But people have taken to using the two terms interchangeably since so many have a router at home to connect to the Internet that doubles as a local hub for a home LAN.

The typical twisted pair LAN uses RJ-45 connectors (the 8 wire phone connectors) for 100BaseT and 1000BaseT (Gigabit). You're not very likely to encounter 10BaseT anymore unless you're servicing a small business or home office that hasn't updated anything in twenty years. Network hubs often give you the choice of a straight through uplink port or a crossover port for daisy chaining. It doesn't matter which one you use as long as you have the right cable. Straight through cables in 100BaseT world have 1-1 correspondence right through the connector, but the pairs are shared between 1 and 2, 3 and 6, 4 and 5, 7 and 8. It's based on the AT&T 258A spec, don't ask why. Crossover cables allow you to connect two PCs without a router or hub in the middle. Crossover cables are wired so the 3 and 6 pair on the first end go to the 1 and 2 pair on the second end, while the 1 and 2 pair on the first end go to the 3 and 6 pair on the second end. The other two pairs aren't always used, and they don't change in the basic crossover cable.

All modern motherboards include the network adapter in the I/O core, but they don't all include the status LEDs and the LEDs may be difficult to see with all the other cables in the way. Network cards generally had one or more exposed LEDs on the exterior to show the link status and network traffic, but being on the back of the case which is often buried in office furniture, they aren't always visible. If the link status LED isn't green, it means there's an open circuit between the network port and the hub, unless the cable is simply made wrong. An open circuit doesn't always mean a broken wire or connector, it could be the distance is just too great. Since you only have one network port in the PC, try swapping the other end of the cable to another hub or patch panel port in the wiring closet. If you encounter an ancient coaxial network running thin Ethernet, make sure there are 50 Ohm terminators at the end of any run. You're highly unlikely to encounter fiber-optic network cables in a home LAN.

If the LAN supports multiple PCs and the others work, have you carefully noted all of the settings for the workstation software from a PC without connection problems and transferred those settings to the problem PC? Generally speaking, everything except the IP address, the workstation name, and the group name (if there is one) should be the same for similar workstations. Especially when setting up new PCs it's easy to make a spelling mistake that prevents the workstation from joining the network. Software troubleshooting for networks is a subject for many thousand page books, so eliminate all of the hardware possibilities before you make yourself nuts.

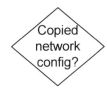

For Windows computers, does Device Manager report any problems with the network adapter? If the network adapter isn't detected or if a problem is reported, the first thing to do is reboot, reinstall the driver, and see if it clears up. In some cases, it may help to disable the motherboard network adapter in CMOS Setup (or remove the old network card) and shut down, go through a reboot cycle, shut down again, re-enable the integrated network adapter (or reinstall the card), and then try reinstalling the device driver. If Windows still doesn't detect the adapter, it's either bad, incompatible, or there's a hardware resource conflict. For older PCs, try the flowchart for troubleshooting hardware conflicts, but for motherboard integrated network ports, all you can do is to make sure the driver and BIOS are up to date.

Have you tried a different port on the hub? Individual ports on hubs can fail at any time, even without the link LED going out on the hub. If there are other PCs on the LAN that are working, swap their cables at the hub and see if the problem follows the port. If there aren't any other PCs on the hub (likely a home router), just try another port.

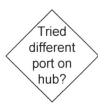

Can you associate the problems with peak usage periods for the network? If the problems only show up when everybody is working on Friday payroll processing or watching Internet videos at lunch, odds are it's just a bandwidth issue and you either need a faster network or to split the existing network in two. If the network runs a mix of 1000BaseT and 100BaseT adapters, it's worth updating everybody to Gigabit, even if it means sticking PCI network adapters in older PCs that have 100BaseT integrated on the motherboard.

Are you sure the problems only show up when the PC is using the network? If the PC is having trouble all the time, you're really on the wrong troubleshooting flowchart. Run the usual anti-virus and anti-malware software to make sure the operating system hasn't been compromised, and then start back at the beginning of the troubleshooting series, especially the motherboard, CPU and RAM and hard drive troubleshooting flowcharts.

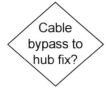

In an office environment, it's useful to make up one super long bypass cable that you can use to connect any PC directly to the hub or patch panel for the sake of testing. In the home environment, you still want to test the PC with a different network cable, so if your cabling is in-wall, move the PC to the same room as the hub or router and test it there. If this fixes the problem, either the other cable, in-wall or out, is bad, or there was some extremely strong electrical field in the routing path of the other cable causing unacceptable levels of noise.

Did you try swapping in a cheap PCI network adapter or a USB Ethernet adapter? Both USB and PCI network adapters are available for less than $10, so it makes sense to swap in a PCI network adapter to make sure the existing add-in adapter or motherboard network support hasn't failed or developed a driver incompatibility after some operating system software update. You may have to disable the motherboard network adapter in CMOS to get the new one recognized. At this point, we've eliminated the physical layer of the network as being the problem, so if the PC can't connect with a proven replacement adapter, the problem is software settings.

Does Windows see the wireless network listed in its connection manager software? If not, start by making sure the wireless adapter in the PC is actually enabled in software, and if there's a switch on a USB WiFi adapter, it's turned on. Next, make sure the wireless router has the wireless enabled by checking the LED on the router, and confirm it's live by using any other WiFi device, like a Kindle, iPad or laptop. If this is a corporate WiFi network, there's a good chance it's hidden (the router has been set not to announce itself) and you will need to get the exact settings from the network administrator to access it. Make sure that the PC wireless adapter is in range and has a decent path to the router. The frequencies used are easily reflected by some construction materials and absorbed by human bodies, and it's not unusual to find that the WiFi connectivity strength (in bars)

to a PC in a room remote from the wireless router drops to nothing if you sit between the PC and the open door.

If this is a home network, do yourself a favor and turn off network security for a test to see if the PC can connect to the unsecured network. The most common wireless connectivity issue in homes and small offices is when somebody is sure they know the network password but they've misremembered or written it down incorrectly. Accidentally using a capital letter at the start of a name which was lower case for the password is a common error. If the PC connects with no security, you know the issue is either the password or the protocols supported.

The vast majority of wireless routers for home networks also offer at least one RJ-45 port for wired Ethernet. If the router has a port and you have a cable, try connecting your PC directly and testing if Windows can at least see the network. Most Windows based PCs don't require any special setup for direct connection to a router and the WiFi password isn't required when plugged directly in with a cable, so you should be able to access the web through a browser.

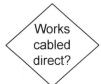

Check again that the wireless router is really enabled by finding the network with any other WiFi enabled device, such as a laptop, iPad or Kindle. If the WiFi network isn't putting out a signal, try running the setup DVD again, the one that was sold with the router. If the router insists that it's alive (its wireless LED is lit and blinking) and the software doesn't report any problems, it could be that it was setup with wireless MAC addresses for security and the other devices connected to it have already had their MAC address registered. The MAC address is a unique hardware identifier that appears on the label of the device, and if your router has MAC screening enabled, you'll have to add the MAC address of your wireless adapter to the list before it will allow your PC to connect.

Have you restored the default settings on the router? There are usually two ways to do this, either through the software that ships on DVD with the router, or a hardware reset button accessed through a little hole on the back or bottom of the router for if you lose the access password you created during the previous setup. If you restore the default settings and neither wired nor WiFi connections work, either the router is bad or the incoming network line you are trying to access (normally the Internet) is down. See the Modem Failure flowchart.

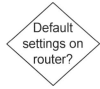

If the PC loses the WiFi signal or if downloads and network access seem to take forever, you first need to troubleshoot whether the problem is in your PC hardware, the router, or an incompatibility or distance limitation between the two. If the WiFi connectivity strength shown by Windows is always low (one or two bars), move the PC and the router closer together for better signal strength before proceeding.

If other PCs or WiFi devices work fine on the network, try updating the device driver for your WiFi adapter before replacing it. For PCs with built-in WiFi on the motherboard, disable it in CMOS and try a USB WiFi stick or an add-in adapter. If no WiFi devices can connect to the network and you've gone through all of the troubleshooting steps above, either the router is bad or the network you are trying to connect to is down.

If all of the devices on your wireless network aren't using the same (and ideally the latest) version of the 802.11 standard, update them if possible. At least your PC and your wireless router should be running wireless "n" or one of the newer replacements, "b" is obsolete and "g" is just good enough for a moderate laptop. If your router and PC wireless adapter are both wireless "n" or better and it's still slow, make sure that you aren't carrying freeloaders on your network by securing it with a password.

If you can borrow a laptop and use the WiFi network without speed problems, it's pretty likely that the issue is the overall performance of your PC which may be running too many tasks or bogged down with malware. If performance lags at times and is fine at other times and your network is secured, it's likely that an Internet connected router is having modem performance issues, and you should see the Modem Performance flowchart. There's always the possibility of interference if your trouble periods are fit into well defined time period, like when somebody is talking on the wireless phone in the house. You can't rule out failing wireless hardware, so if you have multiple devices using the wireless router without problems, you can try swapping the PC WiFi adapter.

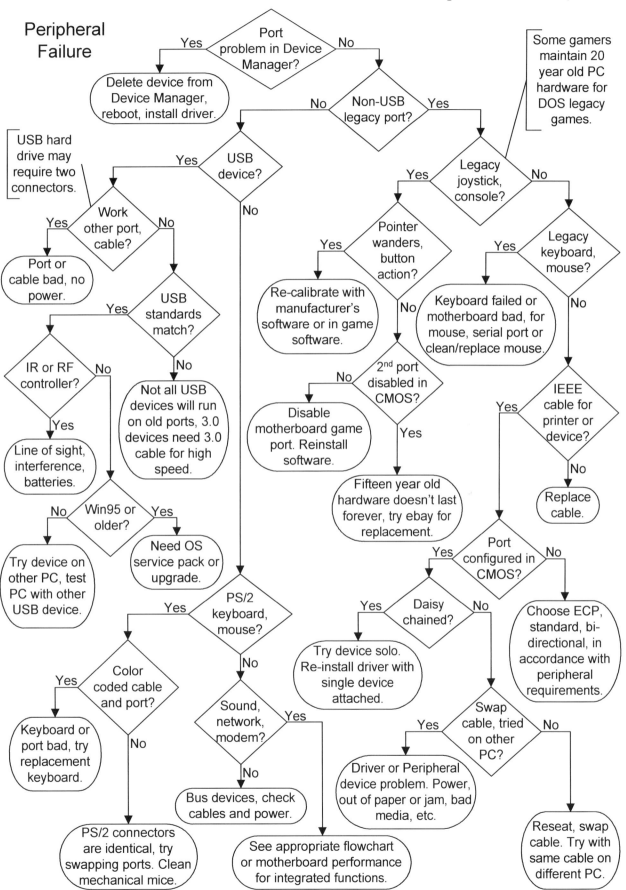

Peripheral Failure

Port problem in Device Manager?
- Yes → Delete device from Device Manager, reboot, install driver.
- No → Non-USB legacy port?

USB hard drive may require two connectors.

Some gamers maintain 20 year old PC hardware for DOS legacy games.

Non-USB legacy port?
- No → USB device?
- Yes → Legacy joystick, console?

USB device?
- Yes → Work other port, cable?
- No → PS/2 keyboard, mouse?

Work other port, cable?
- Yes → Port or cable bad, no power.
- No → USB standards match?

USB standards match?
- Yes → IR or RF controller?
- No → Not all USB devices will run on old ports, 3.0 devices need 3.0 cable for high speed.

IR or RF controller?
- Yes → Line of sight, interference, batteries.
- No → Win95 or older?

Win95 or older?
- No → Try device on other PC, test PC with other USB device.
- Yes → Need OS service pack or upgrade.

PS/2 keyboard, mouse?
- Yes → Color coded cable and port?
- No → Sound, network, modem?

Color coded cable and port?
- Yes → Keyboard or port bad, try replacement keyboard.
- No → PS/2 connectors are identical, try swapping ports. Clean mechanical mice.

Sound, network, modem?
- Yes → See appropriate flowchart or motherboard performance for integrated functions.
- No → Bus devices, check cables and power.

Legacy joystick, console?
- Yes → Pointer wanders, button action?
- No → Legacy keyboard, mouse?

Pointer wanders, button action?
- Yes → Re-calibrate with manufacturer's software or in game software.
- No → 2nd port disabled in CMOS?

2nd port disabled in CMOS?
- No → Disable motherboard game port. Reinstall software.
- Yes → Fifteen year old hardware doesn't last forever, try ebay for replacement.

Legacy keyboard, mouse?
- Yes → Keyboard failed or motherboard bad, for mouse, serial port or clean/replace mouse.
- No → IEEE cable for printer or device?

IEEE cable for printer or device?
- Yes → Port configured in CMOS?
- No → Replace cable.

Port configured in CMOS?
- Yes → Daisy chained?
- No → Choose ECP, standard, bi-directional, in accordance with peripheral requirements.

Daisy chained?
- Yes → Try device solo. Re-install driver with single device attached.
- No → Swap cable, tried on other PC?

Swap cable, tried on other PC?
- Yes → Driver or Peripheral device problem. Power, out of paper or jam, bad media, etc.
- No → Reseat, swap cable. Try with same cable on different PC.

Peripheral Failure - 143

Peripheral Failure

Is the port to which your peripheral is hooked up present and healthy in Device Manager? You can access Device Manager a half dozen different ways in most Windows operating systems, but the most straightforward (no right clicking, etc.) is to go through Control Panel > System. If there are any notations next to the ports in Device Manager, such as "!" or "?", there's a conflict or a problem with the driver. Try deleting the device from Device Manager, rebooting, and letting Windows find and reinstall it. If it's not a standard device, you'll need the driver from the manufacturer. All of the standard I/O ports in modern PCs are integrated on the motherboard, so unless you've upgraded with an add-in adapter, that means using default Windows drivers or re-installing the motherboard drivers.

Are you troubleshooting a non-USB legacy device? Legacy ports started disappearing from PCs around fifteen years ago, though some motherboard I/O cores and add-in adapters preserved them for years in order to support existing peripherals, such as expensive printers. There are a number of converter products for USB to serial ports or for parallel port printers, scanners, other IEEE 1284 peripherals, but that doesn't mean you'll be able to get the old software drivers to work in new Windows versions. While the industry lacks a precise definition for "legacy" it implies "obsolete" so any ports that appear in today's motherboard I/O cores or on standard add-in adapters are not legacy.

Diehard classic gamers would have complained if we dropped all mention of game port joysticks and controllers from these diagnostics. Before USB appeared, most gaming devices were connected to the PC via a 15 pin dedicated gaming port that commonly appeared on the super IDE card, sound card or integrated on the motherboard.

If the pointer or action figure wanders off in one direction when you aren't touching the joystick or controller, it needs to be calibrated. This was often carried out from within the particular game, though more sophisticated controllers came with their own calibration software. If recalibrating doesn't stop drift, it means the stick or controller isn't returning to the neutral position, likely a mechanical failure, but you can try taking it apart and cleaning it, checking for any broken springs or bushings, though you'd have to scavenge for replacement parts.

Are you getting unexpected results from the buttons on the joystick or controller? Either the game or the joystick software should support procedures for assigning buttons, etc. However, older games with limited Windows or DirectX support may simply not work later generations of devices that didn't emulate the original joysticks. Try using the "Game Controllers" tab in Windows Control Panel to configure and test the device.

Is there more than one game port on the PC? One of the problems with game ports appearing on IDE cards, on some sound cards and also integrated on some motherboards, is you could end up with multiple game ports in a single PC when you only had one device to connect. It's usually easier to disable the old motherboard game port in CMOS Setup than to figure out the jumper settings on the super IDE card. After doing so, you may have to reinstall the drivers for the sound card or super IDE card (if they exist) to make Windows aware of the port.

If the joystick works with some other game, the problem is with the compatibility of the joystick with the particular game software. The most advanced gaming controllers that used game ports were highly dependent on their driver software because they reprogrammed the ports to use the available pins for proprietary signaling. The standard I/O address range for game ports was 200 – 20F, meaning 16 bits were set aside. Strangely enough, you can still buy PCI sound cards with 15 pin game ports for a song. For a legacy replacement joystick or controller, you'll have to try ebay.

Legacy keyboards featured a large round connector that attached to what was once the only port integrated on the motherboard. Legacy mice used the 9 pin serial port, though they could connect to the 25 pin serial port with an adapter. The 25 pin serial port was male, to differentiate it from the 25 pin parallel port, which was female. Either could be adapted to a different configuration through a converter plug.

If your known good keyboard (tested it on another old PC or with an adapter on a new PC) doesn't work, it usually means the keyboard controller, commonly called the keyboard BIOS chip, was blown. Some of these were soldered on the motherboard, some were socketed, so if the keyboard connector hasn't broken from the motherboard and all the leads to the motherboard are intact, you can either try replacing the chip or look for a replacement motherboard on ebay. Old mechanical mice can be cleaned, just concentrate on the rollers, not the ball.

Are you using an IEEE standard cable to attach your printer, scanner or other parallel port peripheral? If you've been scavenging cables to get an old peripheral going on a 25 pin parallel port, the cable you found may look just like an IEEE 1284 printer cable, but there were many cables that used the same connectors with proprietary wiring and different missing connections. Either find a cable with molded ends and IEEE 1284 stamped on it, buy a new cable, or look up the pin-out on Wikipedia and ring out every pin with a multimeter. If your peripheral requires a non-standard cable and you don't have it, you can always build one from scratch, given the correct pin-outs. The old 9-pin and 25-pin serial ports were used by "dumb" terminals, old digital cameras, and of course, external dial-up modems.

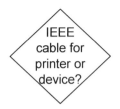

Have you checked the port configuration in CMOS Setup? Depending on the age of your BIOS, you may have the option to select the standard (old fashioned) mode, bi-directional or ECP. The documentation with your printer or parallel port peripheral will tell you whether or not you need to set a specific mode in CMOS Setup. If your ports are not integrated on the motherboard, they are most likely included on an old SIDE (Super IDE) controller, but the settings for these are set by jumpers on the card, and unless the settings are silk screened next to the jumpers, you'll never find them. You should be able to find a PCI card that supports serial ports for old terminals if your ports have failed and you are absolutely desperate to keep an old Unix terminal system running.

Is your parallel port device daisy chained? This was pretty popular with printers and scanners before USB took over, and it was often problematic. The order you installed the devices and the drivers could make a difference, and some printers and scanners wouldn't work on the same port no matter what you did. The best test is to uninstall the drivers for any parallel port peripherals installed, reboot, then try installing the problem device as stand-alone on the port.

Have you tried swapping the cable? Even if it's a molded cable, 100% guaranteed and IEEE compliant, it could be bad or have crushed conductors. Cables pass much of their lives behind desks and on floors, so it's also quite possible that the cable has been damaged. Make sure you do all the idiot checks, like

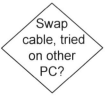

confirming that the peripheral's external power is plugged in to a good outlet. In the end, the best way to test whether a peripheral has failed or whether it's a port or software problem is to try installing it on another PC.

Laser printer not ready errors are commonly paper related - too much, too little or jam. Too much paper in your laser printer input tray can cause continual input jams, or even a "No Paper" error. Not enough paper can also cause a "No Paper" error, particularly on top fed lasers. Paper jams that won't go away or repeat after you clear the old paper are often due to teeny bits of paper torn off and jammed in the paper travel path. Using paper that's too flimsy or too damp can increase these problems.

Inkjet printer paper problems are often caused by too much paper in the hopper. But the most common reason for an inkjet to refuse to print is an empty inkjet cartridge. Other problems are ink cartridges not fully seated, forgetting to remove the protective tape from a new cartridge, and the usual cable and port issues. Out of warranty inkjet repair isn't even worth thinking about unless you paid several hundred dollars for a business version. Replacement printers with rebates are often cheaper than cartridges.

Is the peripheral a USB device? USB is the primary way modern peripherals are attached to PCs, and it's also the most idiot proof. The cables for standard devices can only be plugged in one way and the ends aren't reversible. The flat rectangular end of the cable plugs into the PC and the square end plugs into the device. Both connectors on the cable have an "up" side, normally the USB symbol is molded on the top. If you absolutely force a connector in upside-down, you can break the port.

If you have more USB devices than ports, you can add an external USB hub to provide more ports. However, some USB devices (those without their own power supply) are actually powered by the PC through the USB port and may not work if they are connected through a hub port that doesn't meet that power demand. If you are having a problem with a device connected through a hub, try connecting it directly to a USB port on the PC.

USB peripherals such as printers, scanners and DVD recorders, which require much more power than a whole flock of USB ports could provide, have their own cords and plugs. Make sure any independently powered USB peripheral is turned on and not in an error mode, it should have at least one status LED or readout, before worrying the PC side of the equation.

The first step when you're having trouble with any USB peripheral is to try it on a different USB port, and then swap the USB cable if it still doesn't work. Some USB peripherals that require more power than a single USB port can provide feature two USB connectors for connection to two ports, though the second connector skips the data wires. USB ports mounted on the motherboard can fail mechanically or electrically, and it's not unusual to break a port clean off the motherboard or have the plastic insulator fall out after somebody trips over the cord to the printer. If any of the USB ports show a problem in Device Manager, deleting them and letting Windows reinstall them on the next boot may help. If you're using a USB keyboard for the first time on an older system with PS/2 ports, make sure the USB keyboard is enabled in CMOS Setup.

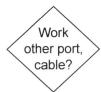

Do the USB standards match? The most recent version of USB is 3.0, while many PCs still in use sport USB 2.0 or even USB 1.1 ports. While a USB 3.0 or 2.0 port should support older devices, a new USB peripheral may not work on an older USB port due to speed or power considerations. For Blu-ray or DVD recorders, the speed is a real issue since buffer underruns can ruin the disc you're recording. For hard drives and many other devices, as long as the USB port supplies sufficient power, they'll usually just run at a slower data speed. But it makes no sense to hang a USB 3.0 SSD drive on a slower USB port, the performance will be a tenth or less of what you paid for even if it works. High speed USB 3.0 devices require a 9 conductor USB 3.0 certified cable to achieve their stated performance.

Infrared (IR) and Radio Frequency (RF) USB peripherals are becoming increasingly common. The wireless mice you see are using a USB connected RF transceiver, as are wireless headphones. 3D glasses for gamers can be wired directly to the PC using a USB cable, or they can be operated by a USB connected IR controller. Whenever an IR or RF device has problems, the first step is to make sure the USB cord for the base station is plugged in and that the software drivers are installed. The usual fail point for wireless mice, headphones and 3D glasses, is the battery. All peripherals need to get their power from somewhere, and if they aren't connected by wire, that means batteries. A clear line-of-site between an IR controller and the peripheral is also required. Your 3D glasses won't

operate if you've covered the USB connected controller with your hat or put a cup of coffee in front of it.

If you aren't running an antique with Windows 95 or older, the last test is to install the peripheral on a different computer and see if it works there. If it does, you know that the problem is either due to the software installed (the application or the driver, which may be incompatible with your OS version) or port failure. You can confirm port failure by borrowing some other known good USB device, like a memory stick, and seeing if that works on any of your USB ports. If not, as long as you have an open expansion slot in the PC, you can buy a PCI adapter with the latest USB technology.

The original version of Windows 95, release 1 or version A, doesn't support USB. The fastest way to determine the Windows 95 version is to right-click on My Computer and display System Properties. Even if you have physical USB ports on the motherboard or on an add-in adapter, you need to upgrade your Windows version to support USB. Windows 95 versions B and C do support USB, though you may have to manually install a few files to get it to work, and '95 is no longer supported by Microsoft. The instructions for adding USB support to versions B and C of Windows 95 are too long to include here, but can be easily found by doing an Internet search with the keywords: "Windows 95 USB upgrade."

Is the problem with a PS/2 keyboard or mouse? These are identified by their small, circular connectors with six metal pins and a rectangular plastic tab for alignment. There are actually USB to PS/2 converters you can buy for a buck or two if your PC has PS/2 ports, you need to replace a mouse or a keyboard, and you can only find USB replacements. The advantage of using the USB to PS/2 converter is that it saves the USB ports for other peripherals.

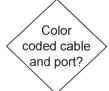

Are the mouse and keyboard ports color coded? The PS/2 connectors used on mice and keyboards can be accidentally plugged into the wrong port, which is particularly easy to do if you're working under a desk. If you mix up the mouse and the keyboard, Windows will usually complain that no mouse is present when it loads. Keyboard connectors are coded purple, mouse connectors are coded green. If the ports aren't color coded, there should be little mouse and keyboard symbols pointing out which is which. If you have the connector fully seated in the correct port and the keyboard or mouse is undetected or doesn't work, replace it.

Mechanical mouse performance degrades over time as the rollers pick up lint. A mechanical mouse can be cleaned by popping the retaining plate off the bottom, dropping the ball out in your hand, and picking the lint off the rollers. Keyboards can fail mechanically, as in keys falling off or sticking, or simply from the letters wearing off the keys. If you think your keyboard electronics have died, try it on another PC before ditching it.

Cleaning a mechanical mouse:

www.fonerbooks.com /r_mouse.htm

If you're having problems with speakers, microphones, headphones, your network or modem, these may be termed peripherals (except for the network) but we deal with them on their own flowcharts in this book. The ports and controllers for the sound, network and dial-up modem will usually be integrated on the motherboard in recent PCs, so you should refer to the motherboard performance flowchart as well.

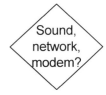

Sound, network, modem?

The remaining types of peripherals are bus attached devices which are rarely seen in home PCs. These include external SCSI drives, external SATA drives, PCI and PCIe expansion boxes, and they usually require a special add-in adapter. In some cases, a cable might be run a very short distance out of the case and be attached to the motherboard controller for a RAID in an externally powered cage, or for a second DVD or Blu-ray recorder in a powered cage that a small PC case doesn't have an open bay to accommodate. In all of these instances, you should double check that the external power source (usually a transformer brick) is active and putting out the proper voltage, and that the cable lengths don't exceed the maximums allowed for the bus type.

SAS RAID and Legacy SCSI Failure

SAS RAID and Legacy SCSI Failure

Are you using a SAS (Serial Attached SCSI) adapter? SAS has replaced traditional SCSI in all modern applications, but SCSI was popular in high performance PCs and PC based servers before SATA came along. SAS adapters can usually work with SAS drives and SATA drives, both being serial bus devices, the difference is mainly in software. SAS drives can run higher signaling voltage, allowing for longer cable lengths.

Is your SCSI adapter recognized by the BIOS at power up? All modern SCSI (pronounced "skuzzy") adapters carry their own SCSI BIOS that must be recognized and loaded at boot time. There are some ancient "dumb" SCSI cards kicking around for running scanners or old CD drives which are run through an operating system driver, but I've never seen a PCI version. When the SCSI adapter BIOS loads, it will flash an on-screen message, like "Press CTRL-A" to access the SCSI BIOS (Adaptec).

SCSI adapters are pretty sophisticated, practically single board computers. There are still some of 5V PCI SCSI adapters kicking around in old business servers, but new PCI slots only support 3.3V adapters. This is the first thing to check in the documentation of your SCSI adapter and motherboard if you've done a motherboard replacement.

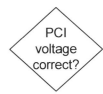

Have you tried moving the adapter to a new slot? Make sure you screw in the hold-down screw and that the card is evenly seated in the slot. The sophistication of SCSI adapters makes them a little more finicky than other PCI adapters, and the order in which the PC BIOS reckons them up may make a difference. You can go into CMOS Setup and play with the PCI bus legacy settings if the adapter BIOS won't load. Quality SCSI adapters are equipped with an onboard LED to confirm the adapter status and report error codes. If you can't get the adapter to report in on power up, proceed to Conflict Resolution.

Does the BIOS screen generated by the SCSI Adapter list any of the SCSI devices you have installed? If the SCSI support is integrated on the motherboard, this information may be combined with the standard BIOS boot screen. The device should be identified by manufacturer, model, SCSI ID and LUN (Logical Unit Number, largely irrelevant unless you're building a

large array). The SCSI adapter itself should appear in this accounting, generally on SCSI ID 7.

Does the SCSI BIOS see all of the SCSI devices you've installed? If it does, whatever access problem you're having is most likely the result of outdated operating system drivers or SCSI application software. If everything works fine but you have intermittent SCSI problems, proceed as if you had answered "no" to this question, and pay special attention to termination, cable quality and SCSI limit issues.

Are all of your SCSI device IDs unique? It's almost certain that you believe they are unique since you set them before you installed the SCSI devices, but double check. The most common failing that can leave you with two devices sharing the same SCSI ID is a misplaced or defective jumper. It's not the black plastic that makes the connection, it's the little metal spring clip within the plastic housing. If the jumper is defective, it won't set the ID bit. Some SCSI jumpers are so tiny that it's easy to miss one of the pins when you place them. If you were trying to set two drives on SCSI addresses "0" and "2" and the jumper on the ID 1 pair missed one of the posts, you'd end up with two drives set to ID 0.

Although the binary addressing should be fully explicated in your SCSI documentation, you're probably working with old stuff for which the documentation is long gone and may not even exist on the Internet, so the general deal is as follows.

Older, "Narrow" SCSI controllers supported up to 8 devices (including the controller), so they required three ID bits to select a unique set of addresses. The standard is to label these as, ID 0, ID 1, and ID 2, where ID 0 is the low bit. An "X" represents a jumper.

Addr	ID 2	ID 1	ID 0
0	0	0	0
1	0	0	X
2	0	X	0
3	0	X	X
4	X	0	0
5	X	0	X
6	X	X	0
7	X	X	X

Newer, "Wide" SCSI controllers and devices support up to 16 addresses, where the controller takes up one, so a single controller can support 15 devices. The only difference between the jumper setting for new and old devices is that newer devices have a fourth SCSI ID selection, ID 3, which is jumpered for addresses 8 - 15. The lower ID bits are set exactly as above, but you add 8 to each address when ID 3 is jumpered.

Is the SCSI bus terminated on both ends? This has gotten particularly tricky since more recent SCSI adapters could auto-sense termination requirements and handle it themselves, and the newer (but still old) LVD scheme provides termination on one end of the cable. The newer SCSI devices that work with the Wide LVD cable should ship with termination disabled, though they may have onboard termination available for compatibility with the older SCSI technology. You really need to check the documentation or hop onto the manufacturer's website for details about the SCSI termination for particular devices.

The important thing to know about SCSI termination is that both ends of the bus must be terminated. The bus is a physical thing, not a theoretical conception. All of the devices on a SCSI bus share the same parallel transmission line for data and signals, and the devices at both ends of the line (or the line itself) must provide termination. There are four basic possibilities for the SCSI bus architecture.

1) You have an internal SCSI adapter and one or more internal SCSI devices. The devices are attached to the SCSI adapter by a ribbon cable. The SCSI adapter is at one end of the bus and must have termination enabled or set on automatic (usually done through the SCSI BIOS, but the oldest SCSI adapters employed a physical jumper). The SCSI device at the end of the bus must be terminated if you're using a 50 wire ribbon cable, or it must be attached to the last connector before the terminator on the end of a 68 wire LVD cable.

2) You have an internal SCSI adapter and one or more external SCSI devices. The SCSI adapter must be terminated, and the last external SCSI device on the daisy chain must be terminated. Some external SCSI devices are equipped with a termination switch, others require installation of a SCSI terminator on their outgoing SCSI connector.

3) You have one or more internal SCSI devices and one or more external SCSI devices, all attached to the same internal SCSI

adapter. The last external device on the daisy chain must be terminated and the last internal device on a 50 pin ribbon cable must be terminated or attached to the last connector on the 68 wire LVD cable. The adapter must have termination disabled because it is in the middle of the bus.

4) You combine any of the above scenarios with a SCSI adapter that supports two internal SCSI busses, a high speed 68 wire LVD bus and an older 50 pin bus. If you have both types of SCSI devices, it's recommended that you install them on separate cables for best performance, even though adapters or dual connectors may be available for the device. Any time you have two internal cables attached to the SCSI adapter, they must be terminated according to their type. The last connector on the 50 wire cable must be connected to a terminated drive, while the last connector on the 68 wire LVD cable must be connected to an unterminated drive.

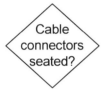

Are all of the cable connectors seated? When you start getting up to 50 pins mating into an old fashioned connector, it can take a bit of pushing. After you think the connector is seated, push on each end of the connector in turn to make sure that it isn't rocking on an obstruction in the middle. A properly seated cable connector won't move, wherever you push on it. The newer 68 pin LVD connectors make the connection in a smaller form than the older 50 pin connectors, and the unfortunate side effect is that the pins themselves are more fragile. Be careful when seating the connectors, and if you have to pull the connector off for troubleshooting, inspect the pins to make sure none are bent over.

Have you obeyed all the SCSI limits? These limits are entirely dependent on the SCSI adapter and devices you are using, not to mention the number of devices on the bus and the type and quality of the cables. Ultra SCSI 160, 320 and 640 have focused on data throughput rather than increasing the maximum bus length. The limitations subject is far too complicated for this discussion, but keep in mind it works both ways. For example, if you build your own cables, you can't put the connectors two inches apart just to keep the cabling in your case neat. There are minimum as well as maximum distances involved, depending on the SCSI technology and the speed at which you are running the bus.

Have you replaced the cables? SCSI cables are the weak links in older machines, particularly when you've made and unmade the connectors a number of times. The stress relief on the connector can fail, particularly if you use the cable to pull the connection apart. Pushing the two halves back together just doesn't cut it in high speed communications.

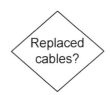

Can you get the adapter to recognize a single device? If the adapter termination is on automatic, you can try putting it on manual and forcing termination on, though it's rarely the issue. If you're using an older Narrow SCSI device for the test, make sure it's terminated. If you're using a Wide device on an LVD cable, make sure it's unterminated and connected to the last connector on the terminated end of the LVD cable. If you can't get the SCSI adapter to see the device, try another one, if you have one available. SCSI adapters ship with pretty good onboard diagnostics, and there may be a further piece of diagnostic software available on the driver CD or the manufacturer's web site. SCSI adapters are one of the higher quality items in the PC industry, but they do fail, so if you absolutely can't get a SCSI adapter to register a device, even when testing with multiple cables and devices, it's probably dead.

If you get the SCSI adapter working with one or more devices but still have problems, it comes down to process of elimination. If it's a reliability issue, try running the bus at lower speed, or with the slower or older devices temporarily detached. If you never got all of the SCSI devices recognized, try them in different combinations and triple check the IDs, though it's always possible that some devices are good and others are dead.

Is your SAS (Serial Attached SCSI) adapter live and reporting a BIOS screen on boot? All SAS adapters feature their own BIOS which you can access through a hot key combination (CTRL-A for Adaptec) which will show you the status of the adapter, all attached drives, and allow you to control various adapter functions.

If the adapter is not recognized and loading its BIOS, the first step is to reseat it in the slot. Make sure the motherboard PCI version is 2.2 or better, unless it's an early SAS adapter that explicitly states it will run on an older version. Make sure that the number of PCI Express lanes are correct. An SAS x4 adapter requires a PCIe x4 slot. There's no point running an expensive SAS adapter in a lower speed slot than it requires because even if it limped by, you'd just be throwing away your investment in the high performance adapter and drives. And check the adapter maker website for an updated list of hardware the SAS adapter has been tested on, especially motherboards.

Are you using an external enclosure for SAS or SATA drives? Most SAS implementations use external enclosures for grouping large numbers of hard drives that can't fit into a PC case. In fact, if your application doesn't involve at least three or more hard drives, you can probably get better performance cheaper by using solid state drives on a PCIe or SATA controller.

Is a single drive in the enclosure reported as bad? SAS controllers are designed for working with large numbers of external drives in enclosures, and some offer the neat feature of being able to blink the status LED of a particular drive in an enclosure to help you find it. The enclosure itself may be able to identify certain drive failures with a status LED.

If you are having trouble getting any of the drives in an enclosure to work, check the fan-out cable, make sure that the drives, adapter and enclosure are all certified as compatible by the adapter maker, and of course, check the enclosure power. It also pays never to mix SAS and SATA drives in an enclosure, even if the specs appear to support it. It doesn't make any sense to use an SAS enclosure as a dumping ground for random drives when performance and reliability are the only justification for the cost.

Does the SAS adapter BIOS see every drive? If you are having trouble with a single drive, check the connections, try replacing the cable, try swapping the drive power if it doesn't spin up. Download the test software from the drive maker for SAS drives for full diagnostics. SATA drives aren't supported quite as well by the manufacturer's software, but there should be some test software available.

Did an auto rebuild initiated by the RAID result in failure? The time to test your RAID implementation is before it fails, not after, and you should follow the adapter maker's guidelines for testing, don't just pull the power plug on one of your server drives to see what happens. In the event an auto rebuild fails, check the obvious things first, like that the replacement hard drive is at least as large as the failed drive, that it's on the adapter manufacturer compatibility list, that it's the same technology (SAS or SATA), and that it's been initialized.

Otherwise, you'll want to try a manual rebuild after consulting the documentation for your adapter.

Are you using a mixture of SAS and SATA drives? Many SAS controllers support a mix of SAS and SATA drives but that doesn't mean it's a good idea. Sometimes people start with an SAS RAID and get sticker shock when they need to replace a single drive, comparing the SAS to SATA pricing. But there's little reason to invest in an SAS controller and any SAS drives if you're going to end up mixing the technologies, and it can result in compatibility problems, even if the adapter maker states that the drives are supported.

Have you flashed the adapter BIOS? Unless you have specific instructions from the adapter maker that you need to flash the adapter BIOS for compatibility reasons, it's a sort of last ditch measure. The adapter maker is the only source for the BIOS upgrade, and they should also supply a program and detailed instructions for carrying out the update.

If you've already flashed the BIOS and none of the drives in the array are bad, go back to the adapter maker's website and check compatibility of the adapter with the motherboard and with all attached SAS devices, by model and manufacturer. If you've been trying to install drives in a new enclosure, take one out and mount it in the PC just to see if it will function there. The fan-out cables for SAS are the apex of PC cabling, so inspect them carefully and make sure you're using a quality cable.

If all of the hardware is in good working order, at least as far as you can determine by status LEDs and the adapter BIOS reporting for the drives, the problem is likely in the operating system setup. Make sure that the adapter and the operating system have been tested together, that any updated drivers have been installed, and try the adapter maker's support forums. Just because an SAS adapter is new and came with a DVD that included drivers for your operating system doesn't mean they are up to date.

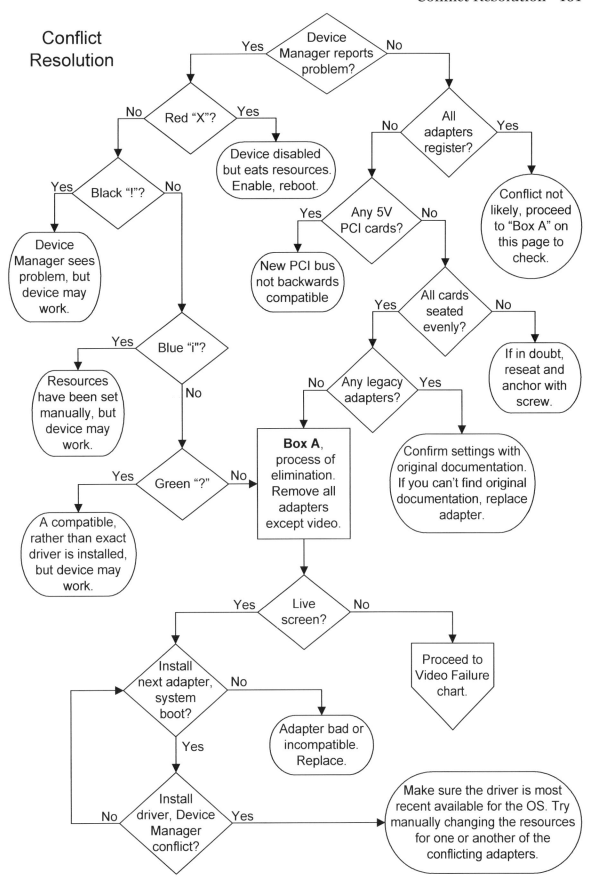

Conflict
Resolution

Device Manager reports problem?

Yes → Red "X"?

No → Red "X"? → **Yes** → Device disabled but eats resources. Enable, reboot.

Red "X"? → **No** → Black "!"?

Black "!"? → **Yes** → Device Manager sees problem, but device may work.

Black "!"? → **No** → Blue "i"?

Blue "i"? → **Yes** → Resources have been set manually, but device may work.

Blue "i"? → **No** → Green "?"

Green "?" → **Yes** → A compatible, rather than exact driver is installed, but device may work.

Green "?" → **No** → **Box A**, process of elimination. Remove all adapters except video.

Device Manager reports problem? → **No** → All adapters register?

All adapters register? → **Yes** → Conflict not likely, proceed to "Box A" on this page to check.

All adapters register? → **No** → Any 5V PCI cards?

Any 5V PCI cards? → **Yes** → New PCI bus not backwards compatible

Any 5V PCI cards? → **No** → All cards seated evenly?

All cards seated evenly? → **No** → If in doubt, reseat and anchor with screw.

All cards seated evenly? → **Yes** → Any legacy adapters?

Any legacy adapters? → **Yes** → Confirm settings with original documentation. If you can't find original documentation, replace adapter.

Any legacy adapters? → **No** → **Box A**

Box A → Live screen?

Live screen? → **Yes** → Install next adapter, system boot?

Live screen? → **No** → Proceed to Video Failure chart.

Install next adapter, system boot? → **No** → Adapter bad or incompatible. Replace.

Install next adapter, system boot? → **Yes** → Install driver, Device Manager conflict?

Install driver, Device Manager conflict? → **No** → (loop back to Install next adapter, system boot?)

Install driver, Device Manager conflict? → **Yes** → Make sure the driver is most recent available for the OS. Try manually changing the resources for one or another of the conflicting adapters.

Conflict Resolution

Does Device Manager report a problem? When you view all of the installed devices by type in Device Manger, a problem is expressed by any extra symbol, like a "!" or a "?" appearing next to a device. If you see a problem, before you shut down and start ripping the machine apart, check if Device Manager can generate a conflict report. Double click on the problem device(s) or click on the little "+" to the left of any questionable devices to get the expanded view. When you double click on any specific piece of hardware in the expanded view and select the Resources tab, there's a little box in the lower half of the results that reports on conflicting devices. Write down any information in the box, rather than trusting it to memory.

Is there a red "X" next to the device that's not working? A red "X" means that the device has been disabled, but it still eats hardware resources and may cause conflicts with other installed devices. This information appears on the "General" tab of Device Manager, the first screen that comes up when you double click on a specific device. At the bottom of the screen there are two check boxes under the heading "Device Usage." If the "Disable in this hardware profile" box is checked, click in the box to uncheck it, then reboot.

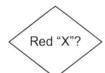

Is there a black "!" next to a device? Device Manager sees a problem, but the device may actually work. It could be that there's a conflict with another device, but the software driver is still capable of managing the input as long as you don't try using both conflicting devices at once. This was fairly common in the days before USB, when running out of Com ports was a common occurrence and sharing Com port IRQs was normal. Even if the device is working, you should check if there's a more recent driver available on the manufacturer's web site.

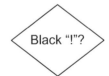

Is there a blue "i" next to a device? An "i" doesn't indicate a problem as much as a warning that the device's resources have been set manually. This could easily be the result of your having cleared up a conflict by manually forcing different resources on a device. If everything works fine, don't worry about it.

Is there a green "?" next to a device? The "?" means that a compatible device driver has been installed. If you're having any problem with a device, the driver is the first thing to check, and running a compatible driver, rather than an exact match from

the manufacturer, is probably at fault. If you can't find the latest version on the web look through all your PC junk for the original driver disk. Unfortunately, I've encountered plenty of modems and the like for which the company had gone out of business and there was no way to find, much less determine, the exact driver for the device. If you have the patience to fool around with installing the generic operating system drivers for the device or downloading and trying close matches from the web, go ahead. If you're doing this for a business, replace the adapter; it's not worth the time.

Do all the adapters register? Is the BIOS or the operating system even aware that the adapter is installed? Even a legacy adapter should be found by whatever software driver or configuration application that it shipped with. If all the adapters are present and accounted for, and Device Manager didn't report any problems, the issue you're trying to diagnose probably isn't a conflict. However, if you've tried everything else, it's always possible, so skip to Box A and begin the process of elimination.

Do you have any 5V PCI cards? Depending on the age of your motherboard, it's probably using one of the newer PCI versions that are not backward compatible with the original 5V PCI cards. The fix for this is to replace the adapter, not the motherboard. The recent PCIe specifications don't include support for 5V signaling, because manufacturers began dropping 5V signaling support from PCI implementations on their own initiative many years ago.

Are all of the adapters seated evenly and secured? Actually, there are some alternative case designs that don't involve anchoring the adapter in place with a screw on the back rail. One approach is to lock all installed adapters in place with a single bar. However, it's not the top of the card but the contact edge you should be looking at. I've encountered plenty of adapters where the circuit board was improperly mounted on the metal bracket. Another possibility is short standoffs under the motherboard and a high rail on the case. If the contact edge of an adapter doesn't seat all the way into a slot and that adapter isn't being registered by the PC, you may have to straighten out the bend at the top bracket to let the card seat all the way.

Do you have any legacy adapters installed? Legacy adapters, whether 8 or 16 bit ISA adapters, 32 bit VESA or EISA, are very questionable in the current plug-n-play environment, even if the motherboard has a slot to accept them. The card may feature physical jumpers or switches for allocating resources, or it may have shipped with a software configuration tool. If you don't have the original documentation, you can try going by the settings printed on the adapter, but I wouldn't waste too much time on it.

Box A. The brute force method to solving hardware conflicts is to begin by eliminating the conflict by eliminating all the optional adapters. Then you begin reinstalling the adapters, one at a time, until the conflict reappears. Not very high tech, but effective. Start by removing all of the add-in adapters except the video card.

Do you get a live screen? The "live screen" referred to in this case is a boot screen generated by the BIOS or an operating system splash screen. It doesn't include any monitor generated messages like "No signal present." If you don't get a live screen, proceed to the Video Failure chart.

Does the system boot? Power down, unplug the system, and install the next adapter. When troubleshooting adapter conflicts, I tend to sequence them by cost, installing the most expensive adapter first. That way, when you do reach an adapter that's causing a conflict, you can try swapping it out with another rather than worrying which adapter is to blame. If installing an adapter actually prevents boot in an otherwise stable system, just replace the adapter.

Install the driver for the device you just installed. Does Device Manager now show a conflict? If not, power down and install the next adapter. If you do get a Device Manager conflict, make sure you have installed the latest possible version of the driver for your operating system by checking the manufacturer's web site. If you are using the latest version of the driver, manually change the setting of the adapter you just installed. If Device Manager won't let you change the individual resource settings, try selecting a different standard configuration, if available. Make sure you have the BIOS defaults set in CMOS Setup.

If that still doesn't do it, return to Box A, strip out all of the adapters except the video and reboot so Windows can reset the registry. Next, start the process again, but this time install the problem adapter first, and find out if the conflict is with the video card or motherboard. If so, replace it. If not, continue with the process, and the operating system may clear the conflict just based on the order the drivers are installed.

Made in the USA
Lexington, KY
30 January 2015